THE TRUE MEANING OF MALCOLM X

by Don Steele

"The True Meaning of Malcolm X" was originally published as a section in **The Revenge of Malcolm X and The Fruits of the Negro Leaders**, Volumes I and II, 1998

Printed in the **Community Voice Newsjournal**, which is distributed in 22 states, from July 1993 - December 1994; "The True Meaning of Malcolm X" was printed from July 16 to December 3, 1993.

THE TRUE MEANING OF MALCOLM X

PART 1[1]

I'm very glad that Malcolm X has been rescued from oblivion and pushed forward by the masses of blacks. It must be noted for the record that this present development certainly is not the wish of those who murdered Malcolm X. This murder of Malcolm X was not just carried out by Black Muslim zealots, concerned with avenging the honor of Elijah Muhammad whom Malcolm X accused of dishonorable behavior with his teenaged secretaries (getting them pregnant and then kicking them out of the Nation of Islam), which one of Malcolm's assassins stated was his reason for killing him. It was also very much the work of the white power structure, bent on destroying a strong black leader who was intent on the liberation of black people. There is every reason to believe, in fact, that the white power structure played an instigating role in fomenting the plot that resulted in Malcolm X being gunned down on February 21, 1965.

I myself had served as a bodyguard for Malcolm X while he was in Detroit one week earlier, February 14, 1965. It was the fourth and last time I'd do so. I was just a teenager, but very much politically involved. I had a keen interest in Malcolm X, although I was never a Muslim and in fact I didn't believe in God at the time. I was an atheist. Like some other radical blacks, I was a Marxist, but I was a black nationalist Marxist. Most of the American Marxists (communists) were whites (there weren't very many of us black

Marxists), and most of them didn't like Malcolm X at all. Later the most famous black Marxists were the leaders of the Black Panther Party and Angela Davis, but the Communist Party USA to which Davis belonged was against black nationalism and Malcolm X. Still later, Stokely Carmichael became a Marxist.

As a matter of fact, at the time of Malcolm's assassination, Malcolm X was perhaps the most feared and hated political figure in America. It wasn't just that Malcolm X was feared and hated by white racists and open bigots. He was hated by the white liberals and the larger portion of white radicals and leftists of every description. Across the entire white spectrum of political views, from left to right, and right to left, Malcolm X was feared and hated by all except a very few.

Nor was it any better among the official "Negro" leadership. Malcolm X was feared and hated by all the civil rights organizations, by all the official leaders, by every black who was dependent on white donations. Then on top of this rejection, the Nation of Islam with Farrakhan as one of the louder voices were castigating to hell Malcolm X, poisoning the atmosphere against him, and making it known, they wanted Malcolm X dead.

So who was left? As far as politically conscious and active elements were concerned, only various radical blacks, mostly nationalists of various descriptions, a few New York celebrities like Ossie Davis, and a few politically isolated, radical whites. But as far as the masses of blacks were concerned, Malcolm X had an appeal among the black working classes of the North. Malcolm X's appeal was to the grassroots. The voiceless little people, who were Malcolm X's own roots.

After Malcolm's assassination, all these elements, white and black, from far right to far left of both races, in an almost unprecedented cohesion, agreement and unholy alliance, worked to castigate, lie, distort, and trample on this man's grave, to assign his memory to some tunnel in hell, which was to be sealed, and never opened. Malcolm X was to be dead. Completely.

It's very important to make these observations, since today matters are quite different. There are many who rush to embrace Malcolm X. There's no black leader who today is more popular and revered. How Malcolm X was hated, how he was lied about, how all the black and white leaders vilified and cursed Malcolm and have done their utmost to bury his memory with his body are points being lost in all the admiration poured onto Malcolm X.

Why has this difference come about? True, Malcolm's autobiography published not long after his death has something to do with keeping his memory alive. How did this book get published when there was such opposition to Malcolm X? Actually, Alex Haley's original publisher withdrew from publishing the book, and the word was out to suppress the book. "The Autobiography of Malcolm X" was, after some searching, first published by Grove Press. Grove Press had a radical stream and was known for publishing such obscene material as the complete writings of Marquis de Sade.

Eventually, my political mentor was contacted to be the editor of the book. "The Autobiography of Malcolm X" was edited by my political mentor in Detroit, and in the household where I then lived, since I had been informally adopted by my political mentor and his wife. Much of the style of the book is due, not to Haley, but to the editing. I know this to be true because I was there. I saw all the heavy changes, corrections, and re-writings that were done to Haley's book to make it what it is today. I read Haley's original manuscript with these corrections and changes. My political mentor, by the way, was a white Marxist, born a Jew.

My political mentor was also the first to publish a volume on Malcolm X's speeches, and published probably the first book on the political analysis of Malcolm X's last year. These are historical facts which should be known, and I write these facts although I today am no longer a Marxist, nor atheist, and haven't been so for nearly 20 years.

But although various literature had been continually published about Malcolm X, and there were still films of him around, this alone did not assure that this overwhelming opposition and formidable alliance by erstwhile political enemies to smother Malcolm X would be defeated. As an immediate conduit for Malcolm's name and life, it was necessary that black radicalism increase in strength, even though black radicalism in all forms of black and cultural nationalism, Pan Africanism, communists, revolutionaries, etc. would not gain the dominant political tide. This militant current most visibly was symbolized by Carmichael and the rise of the Black Power movement on the one hand, and later in the appearance of the Black Panther Party, whose leaders, Newton, Seale, and Cleaver, all traced their political lineage to Malcolm X.

Still, many of these elements considered Malcolm X as just a transitional figure and Huey Newton in particular felt his own image, his own books and writings were the more advanced replacements for Malcolm X. This multifarious black radicalism was a scattered matrix of many different rows and columns, leading to and extending from many different claimants, espousing many different programs, with many different types of group and organizational collections.

All these militant activities by angry and dissident blacks, while more colourful and original, were still outside the mainstream Negro politics, which consisted of the established civil rights organizations, whose symbolizing image was Martin King. While both were ostensibly working towards black liberation from white racist rule, in reality, the two different streams had profoundly different meanings, and, in fact, were enemies of each other. Not brethrens in struggle except on the more shallow and surface levels.

Nevertheless, the various black militant and nationalist groups sputtered and died out as real contenders for political power by the end of the seventies. Various aspects of their militancy and nationalism were absorbed by osmosis by the mainstream Negro current. The official civil rights groups were installed into power, rewarded, and a remake of black cities was effected with blacks making great gains in many economic and social areas. A large black professional class of college educated blacks appeared, and blacks began to take power positions in much larger numbers in institutions and jobs formerly denied to African Americans, including the courts and police departments and higher rankings in the military.

The working class also saw a rise in minimum wages, and it was possible, as with an auto worker, to make more money than a college graduate. Extravagantly high and exorbitant multi-million dollar salaries and royalties began to be earned by black athletes, entertainers and celebrities on a large scale. Black political power has most visibly been noticed in the election of blacks to mayoral positions in major American cities. And throughout the eighties this progress and remaking of America continued. Presently, opening the nineties, black elected officials have added a United States Senator to their list, and a Governor.

So, again, it's to be wondered, how is it that Malcolm X has risen from the ashes when even the black radical movement has dissipated? Why is it that Malcolm X lives? Why have not the successful civil rights organizations, with their image and myth of Martin King, not prevailed in squashing Malcolm X? Why should Malcolm X be of more than just curious interest to so many, at all? Is he just a fad? If so, this fad has continued for years, and its momentum is still increasing.

Concomitant with the ascendancy, and now I can declare, supremacy of Malcolm X's image, has been the decline of Martin King's image and attachment. Again, why is this so? To answer these questions and more is to begin to understand The True Meaning of Malcolm X.

PART 2[2]

In the first article I outlined the fact that when Malcolm X was gunned down in February 1965, he was a hated man. This hatred and opposition were remarkable because they aligned otherwise very hostile political groupings. Both blacks and whites were against Malcolm X and were glad to see him dead! These whites included not just the obvious right wingers, but white liberals and leftists as well, including many communists. This thrill was also shared by blacks of most of the political spectrum, and not just the Black Muslims (Nation of Islam), not just Farrakhan, but Martin King as well. Propriety and the circumstance that Malcolm X was a black leader kept many from expressing too directly their true gladness. But Martin King, in a flippant way, lied and taunted that Malcolm X had just gotten what his teachings taught. (But what did Martin King get with respect to his teachings?)

I also pointed out, for the record, that after Malcolm's assassination, there was a concerted effort by this unholy alliance to, along with his body, bury and seal from consciousness the memory of Malcolm X. Political vultures were set loose to pick and devour Malcolm's political remains, leaving them unrecognizable. I particularly remember Carl Rowan's nasty article. This agent, who worked for a CIA propaganda front in Africa, wondered why anybody should care for Malcolm X, pointing out that Malcolm X had previously been a pimp and thief.

The questions which the reader was left with in the first article were how has Malcolm X risen, Phoenix like, from the oblivion assigned him to become the number one image and most revered of all the black leaders? How is this possible when so much has been spent to prop Malcolm's opponent, Martin King as the blacks' real leader; and when so many economic, social and political gains have been made by blacks under the King banner? How is this possible when hundreds of billions of dollars have been spent, when all the media, both black and white, when all the propaganda, when all the teachings, when every pore of society has been trumpeting and inundating us with King, even as the black radical movement has virtually disappeared, plowed over by elected Negro officials and Big Money, how is it possible, Malcolm X should still move forward, move ahead, and stand alone, towering above all others? How is this possible?

The root answer to this is because of Divine Will. There is no other force that can overcome such objective obstacles. None whatsoever.

However, this explanation of Divine Will, while true, needs to be fleshed out and explained by more earthly references where possible. But such ordinary, earthly, tangible, empirical analyses can never be complete, can never be a full or real explanation, but a pretence in a root explanation. A pretence which just adds material knowledge and information, but which singularly or altogether can never really explain why. Anymore than all the courses in biology, physiology and anatomy can really ever explain, along with all the other natural sciences why a human being?! Why life? Why the universe?

It is with this understanding and caveat that it is the Divine Will which is in the background and the Secret Cause that I offer these more mundane, connecting points referring to black social and political history. In fact, in a subsequent article in this series I will have to return to the Divine Mind to comprehend political events of this century. (The reader may recall that I wrote in the first article that on the different occasions I met Malcolm X while still a teenager, I didn't believe in God. Obviously, my thoughts on this question have changed.)

The simplest explanation for this phenomenon of Malcolm X's ascension is the fact that the black masses, the ones Malcolm X appealed to and addressed, the grassroots, are not pleased with their condition, despite all the progress that's been made by the civil rights organizations. Noticeably, the young who measure their lives from a different starting point than the older African Americans are not satisfied with conditions.

There is an underlying comprehension, only partially surfaced as political consciousness, that these blacks need new leadership, that the Martin King leadership is not really addressing their needs and their concerns. The appearance and expression of Malcolm X is an implicit rejection of Martin King and the programs of the civil rights leaders.

The powers-that-be, both blacks and whites, being unable to stop Malcolm X's forward march into the consciousness of the masses of blacks, have decided to do in this case what they successfully have done before: If you can't beat them, join them.

So, the esablishment has joined the Malcolm X movement with one aim: to co-opt the movement, to steer it into safe channels, to distort and belie the meaning and purpose of Malcolm X, to control it.

This is what happened to the black revolution. It was replaced by the "Negro" revolution, so Malcolm X charged. This is what happened to the March on Washington, Malcolm X averred as an example, where King eventually gave his most celebrated "I Have a Dream" speech. Originally as Malcolm accused in his famous "Message to the Grassroots" speech of 1963, Martin King and the official Negro leaders were not even part of the March on Washington movement.

The March on Washington movement was a radical, black grassroots movement, unled but vibrating through the ghettos of black America. It was a movement to March on Washington in an act of defiance and demand. A March which was to threaten the greatest confrontation in history with white America at its titular seat of power. A March which was to bring Washington to a halt. A March which was to stop the city from governing or moving. A March which was to prevent airplanes from flying and cars from moving, as bodies would be laid on runways and freeways. A March which was to present thousands and tens of thousands and hundreds of thousands of angry, I-don't-give-a-damn-any-more-I'm-tired-of-this-crap black folks! This was the head wind of the black revolution. Of all the nationally known leaders, only Malcolm X supported this mass wave of black protest, this militancy, this defiance.

Seeing what was happening and getting scared, then President John Kennedy called into his office Martin King and the Big Six Negro leaders to have them call the March on Washington off. They pointed out to Kennedy that they couldn't call off the March because they weren't themselves even part of the March. All of this was happening independently of them, and beyond their control. It was at that point, Malcolm X says, that Kennedy decided to co-opt the March, and to place King and the Big Six Negro leaders in charge of the March. He then paid these leaders Cash--what was then a lot of money--to sell out the March on Washington.

From being something radical, hot and defiant, the March on Washington became something pleasant, cool and pleading. Malcolm X, in no uncertain terms, charged Martin King with "a sell out."

The particular efforts to control the Malcolm X movement by the killers of Malcolm X are through various related means. First there's simply the trivialization and obfuscation of Malcolm X's teachings and meaning. This is done by concentrating on his biography in such a way that the prevailing notion is that Malcolm's important lesson is that Malcolm X educated himself by reading books, so simple education is the message! There's also the rush to cash in on his image in a pop culture way, so that his T-shirts are to be compared to an Elvis Presley or Marilyn Monroe T-shirt. A fad. As shallow as a rock or movie star, even if enduring.

Second, there's the effort to paint Malcolm X as just a more radical version of the Negro leaders, the civil rights leaders, with little difference in substance. That Malcolm X was working his way to becoming a moderate like King, since his trip to Mecca opened his eyes to the fact that all whites weren't devils. The lesson of Malcolm X being one may change from being hot and angry, indeed hating whites to loving whites, which was the position of Martin King. Malcolm realized the error of his previous politics, and had seen the true position, which, of course, was King's.

Third, buttressing what has actually been the whites' greatest and most successful Con Game, snaring nearly all concerned, blacks and whites: A Con Game that has portrayed and framed the black struggle as being 95% about the issue of violence versus non-violence. This is how Martin King has been used. Supposedly, it's all about violence vs. non-violence. That Malcolm X's program, which differed little in underlying substance from King's, was meaningfully different only on the question of advocating violence be used against whites. While the Gandhi-like King advocated non-violence. This framing of the struggle by whites has convinced most that this has been the greatest political and social issue facing blacks and separating Martin King from Malcolm X.

All lies, distortions and caricatures usually contain some truths, and the above efforts to control what Malcolm X was about are no exceptions. Anyone can make his own selections from the shifting, changing and dynamic career of Malcolm X to claim what Malcolm X was about. But Malcolm X couldn't have been about, or his meaning couldn't have been about both what his killers claim he was about and have spent so much towards crushing him and his memory versus the needs of the masses of blacks. It's unfortunate that even among those who aren't the ranked hypocrites and pretenders, who truly support and love Malcolm X that such ignorance prevails that no sensible and consistent understanding can be gained from them either. Not even from his immediate family, his wife and daughters, whose love for him can't be questioned. But despite their closeness, they're very far from understanding Malcolm X.

So, lest I also be accused of merely presenting my own distorted account of the True Meaning of Malcolm X, also just selecting out what I want, with the result having no greater entitlement to being accepted as the True Meaning of Malcolm X than anybody else's account, let me separate myself from the rest by presenting two criteria which must prevail. By this I mean that this matter is not just left to whomever has an opinion or two. The matter can be decided by using standards, just as a ruler or gauge or scale is a standard used to measure or weigh items.

The reader is invited to think until the next issue on what such criteria should be in order to gauge The True Meaning of Malcolm X.

PART 3[3]

In Part 2, the reader was left with pondering the criteria to use in gauging The True Meaning of Malcolm X, lest we become just putty in the hands of not only blacks' enemies but ignoramuses and silly people as well. If one were a black basketball star, a boxer or other athlete, then everyone would consider it foolish to place on the same level and weigh with the same importance every interesting aspect of a star's personal biography with what is the true essence and meaning of his stardom. Take Mike Tyson, for example. Whatever traumas he faces in life, whatever outside ring shenanigans, the true meaning of Mike Tyson is not these matters, but Tyson's presence inside the boxing ring, the significance of which is that he's one of the greatest knockout fighters in the history of the sport.

Similarly, with everything else. So too it must be with Malcolm X. Hence, by my demanding that criteria be established is simply in keeping with common sense and practice. But common sense and practice, unfortunately, are not matters one can assume when it comes to questions and answers regarding black liberation and black leaders.

First, it's true all accounts concerning Malcolm X or concerning anybody or anything else will be both a selection process and an interpretation process. This is why, contrary to popular beliefs, there's No Such Thing as "objective reporting." There's No Such Thing as "objective news," or "objective history," or objective anything, really. Just being able to see an object with the eyes involves selecting and interpreting the object. Everybody won't see or interpret the same object the same. That's one of the reasons many people need glasses to see. The selecting and interpreting processes are part of the perceptual organs themselves. This is not something limited to social and political evaluations.

Nevertheless, this doesn't elevate all accounts to being equal in value and truth. That there's no difference in truth value if different people see the same object as a cow or horse or barn. That there's no difference between one person adding 2 plus 2 to get 4, and another adding 2 plus 2 to get 6 or some other number than 4. It is this diffence in truth value that gets the label of "nominal objective." What I'm presenting about Malcolm X, and the first part of any criteria must qualify as the "nominal objective." That is, all that I write can be documented from verifiable sources, and will stand up to any critical scrutiny by any probing body. Plus, there's no selected out facts or information which can be later presented which will alter, much less destroy--which is the case with all other selections and interpretations--what is being presented here.

Second, the real heart of the criteria lies here: the true meaning of Malcolm X does not rest solely and simply with what Malcolm X happened at any given time to have personally believed or done, nor speculations as to what Malcolm X might have done or become. Although these matters can't be ignored, nevertheless, the true meaning of Malcolm X is much greater than Malcolm X's personal biography. Otherwise, there could be little meaning or purpose in seeing Malcolm X as a black political leader.

Given the shallowness of pop culture, this fact cannot be overstated. Malcolm X was not a rock or movie star. Malcolm X's fame and stardom come from the power he put into his progam for the liberation of black people. As such, the basis for any nominally objective selection and interpretation, MUST be based first, foremost and always upon the political "vector" (arrow) which Malcolm X incarnated and from which he drew his strength and power. This is Malcolm X's 'boxing ring,' or 'basketball court.' This political vector did not begin with Malcolm X nor did it end with him. A normal vector (mathmatically defined as a straight line with a direction) requires at least two points. Malcolm X was only one point.

Therefore, every attempt to pontificate about Malcolm X which glaringly neglects this reality is like trying to read a map, or pilot a ship or plane with no axes or coordinates. In mathematics, you can only define something by reference to its coordinates or system; and much of higher mathematics exists in virtue of presenting and working with different types of coordinate or reference systems.

Malcolm X's political vector was NOT simply black freedom fighter, at one with Martin King and the Negro leaders. This is the astonishing ignorance, and dull lazy-mindedness fostered by the black masses' enemies. Malcolm X was the expression, continuation and direction of a line of political thought and effort which have been characterized as black nationalism. This was Malcolm's political vector. Malcolm's own point on the political map must form a straight line with the point of the other great black nationalist leader of this century, Marcus Garvey.

Malcolm X himself even after his split with Elijah Muhammad, even after his trip to Mecca, and right up to the platform and podium at which he was gunned down defined himself still as a black nationalist. The very purpose of Malcolm X's speech that very last day was to elaborate and move on his black nationalist program for the liberation of black people. There's no way Martin King and the Negro leaders who opposed Malcolm X would have defined themselves as black nationalists.

Failure to understand this capital distinction NECESSARILY means to fail to understand The True Meaning of Malcolm X.

For many readers who have read the previous two articles, it may have come as a great surprise and dismay to learn that Martin King was accused by Malcolm X of being "a sell out,"-- Malcolm's words--and being a Negro who was used and paid by whites to stop the black revolution. It came as unwelcomed information that Malcolm X and King were not just two black freedom fighters, both on the same path. It wasn't exactly appreciated to see published the fact that the Negro leaders secretly cheered Malcolm's assassination. That there was great enmity between Malcolm X and the official, white-supported Negro leaders is something they wish not be publicized.

But this is the truth as the documents of the period will prove. I myself know because I was there. I served as a bodyguard of Malcolm X on four separate occasions when he came on visits to Detroit, although I was just a teenager and could only offer my life to save his. Like any good soldier, to save his general. I also was involved in the politics, and knew the discussions, and lived with the man who edited and saw to it Malcolm X's Autobiography was published, and who published the first selection of Malcolm X's speeches, based upon the tapes that were made of Malcolm's speeches, and who published perhaps the first political analysis of Malcolm's last year.

The reason Malcolm X, as stated in the first article, was personally hated by the Negro leaders is not only because Malcolm X had a radical black nationalist agenda for the liberation of blacks, while they had something quite different, although this difference was sufficient for enmity between Malcolm X and them. Their animus was so great because Malcolm X's missiles were fired not just at whites, as many presently are led to believe, but Malcolm X fired nearly as many on them, the quisling Negro leaders. They were Malcolm's targets as well.

Malcolm X was not of the mode or belief of the present Negro leadership, where everyone is covering for the other. What distinguished Malcolm X personally from every other national leader, and this difference eventually would include Elijah Muhammad and those in the Nation of Islam, a difference which would eventually push Malcolm outside of the Black Muslims' organization, is that Malcolm X was the ONLY national leader who was GENUINELY concerned, 100% committed and believing in the liberation of black people! The ONLY one.

The other Negro religious and political leaders had only various degrees of commitment. This commitment ranged from none, absolutely zero with no pretence whatsoever, to perhaps 40% or 50% or even 60% to 70%, absolute tops! By contrast, Malcolm X was 100% committed to blacks' liberation.

How does one measure this difference? By rhetoric? By how many hours one puts in at the office and years of involvement? By the number of speeches one makes? By one's writings? By the number of demonstrations organized and attended? By the number of followers, admirers and believers one has?

These matters indeed are important and necessary gauges, but they really just measure one's involvement. Not one's commitment. All of the Negro leaders could point to having paid their dues in most of the above areas. So could Malcolm X. Yet, there was a fundamental difference in commitment.

This difference in commitment is measured by nothing less than one's attitude towards--THE MONEY!!

Malcolm X, castigating the blacks said, "When they (the white man) drop them dollars on the Negro, his very soul goes." People in general, but blacks in particular, have proven to be very weak when faced with the money from the enemy or from any other source. Thus, Martin King is to be praised and congratulated for separating himself from most of the Southern Negro religious ministers who'd wanted nothing to do with upsetting the racist social arrangements. They were being well paid by their black church constituents. In addition, they had an extra supply of sex from many of the women members; they ate all they wanted, drove Cadillacs, and they held the respect of the community. Their commitment to black liberation was absolutely zero. Many in fact were called upon by whites to openly oppose King and the other civil rights marchers when they came into or near their areas, "upsetting" their black constituents.

From this level of zero commitment to black liberation because of the money and creature comforts these ministers were receiving, plus their fears of bodily harm including death by whites, step by step like a pyramid, the various levels of black commitment were displayed by various leaders and followers. What forced the movement onto the leaders and created new leaders who expressed these momenta was an intangible force that was triggering the masses, breaking out like a disease, first here, then there, bobbing like toboggans, but more and more defining waves, connecting waves, irrepressible surges, social and political storms and cracks, which threatened to reach hurricane scale and eathquake. It was the masses of blacks moving forward, bent on social and political changes. Bent on liberation. But how were these blacks to be channelled?

Knowing that the road King channelled this outburst vs. the road Malcolm X channelled it were two roads which did not both lead to Rome explains both the present black masses' predicament and The True Meaning of Malcolm X.

PART 4[4]

In Part 3, we established the criteria by which Malcolm X must be measured, which is comparable to how one measures a star in any arena, that is, in the actual arena in which that star performs. Therefore, many personal details of Malcolm X's life can't take on the same dimensions of scale or importance than the arena in which Malcolm X fought. For example, the fact that Malcolm X changed from being a pimp and hustler to a freedom fighter is of course interesting but hardly the central issue. The fact that Malcolm X was self-educated is admirable, but not his True Meaning.

Nor is the fact that Malcolm X was for black liberation a sufficient criterion for locating and defining Malcolm X's arena, simply because he'd not have had the same line up of political forces against him as he did. True, Martin King had openly white racists against him, but he had the greatest support and payments from other whites. Martin King received the Nobel Prize because of this white and broad political support, and later, virtual apotheosis after his death, because of this broad white support. By contrast Malcolm X was loathed by and received imprecations from nearly all the political forces, black and white, left and right, and was hoped to be buried for good, not only his body, but his memory and agenda as well.

This criteria is that Malcolm X was a black nationalist. Martin King and the Negro leaders weren't. Programmatically, this meant important differences between Malcolm X and Martin King in breadth and depth and political allegiances. Moreover, these differences are not simply abstract and intellectual and of no substantial consequences--except, as the programming goes, on the question of violence vs. nonviolence. The end results of King's programs, insights and understandings are with us today: The mass murders of blacks on blacks, the overcrowded prisons, the drug addictions, the dropout rates, the teenage pregnancies, the high unemployment, the homelessness, the mean streets, the dependences on government programs, etc. etc. are all the legacies of King. Malcolm X's program was designed to give different results.

Again, it will shock many reades to see any connection between these ill social conditions facing the black masses and the triumph of Martin King's program vis-a-vis the failure of Malcolm X to have his chance. Yet, as I began these series I pointed out that the images of Malcolm X have come up from the masses of blacks, and that Malcolm's name and image represent an implicit, although not fully conscious, rejection of Martin King and the Negro leadership who represent and enforce King's legacies.

I will return to this matter in subsequent articles. But I must continue to explain the other point presented in the last article: the 100% commitment in blacks' liberation as was Malcolm X's versus something much less by others, although in varying degrees, from a commitment level of absolute zero to a high of 50% by some to a rare few who had as much as a 70% commitment. I offered the criterion for measuring this difference being in one's attitude towards the MONEY. The weakness of blacks was not only in the fear of physical bodily harm, but psychologically more prevailing for most was the chance to make or lose money. I stated this is what eventually forced Malcolm X out of the Nation of Islam.

Where I left the reader was the appearance of a "breaking down the racist barriers" mass movement by blacks, who were staging many different demonstrations and protests and forming many different organizations with many different programs and points of view. Most importantly, this was a black movement the white man could not stop.

But why couldn't the white man stop it? Why couldn't he just gun down the blacks, like the South African government did to black protestors in the Sharpsville massacre of 1959?

Now, I must give an analysis and understanding of which a large part was understood in some fashion or another by Malcolm X and what he represented but which was virtually a complete blank with Martin King and what he represented. And since the King forces have won, this analysis and understanding will be something entirely and explosively new to most readers. By the way, it's never been in the interest of whites to let blacks have this understanding, which is another component to why the blacks' oppressors threw their support to Martin King.

To preface this analysis I must point out a FUNDAMENTAL difference from the very beginning between Malcolm X's overall analysis and perception of events versus Martin King's. A difference which very few have recognized or understood, but which was at the very center of Malcolm's political agenda, and which easily and quickly explains his actions after he left the Nation of Islam, as brief as that one last year was.

FUNDAMENTALLY, Malcolm X viewed and understood the black revolution as only a part and parcel of the WORLD WIDE revolutions against the oppression of non-whites by whites. Malcolm X, from the very beginning, had an international perspective and identified himself and blacks in America with a struggle against a worldwide white oppressive system. He identified and linked the African American revolt as just the national part of the worldwide revolts and struggles by all non-whites in the world against white rule around the world. Malcolm X aligned American blacks against these European and American white systems. These other peoples were to be allies and sources of support for blacks in America.

On the other hand, Martin King and the Negro leaders only saw the Negro revolt as purely an American issue. King limited the vision and meaning of the black revolt, even as he limited and gutted it. Naturally, the blacks' oppressors never wanted blacks to identify or see their struggles as part and parcel of this international struggle against white oppressive rule, from the rank colonizations in Africa, Asia and Latin America to the de facto colonization of blacks in America. The King forces even today have restricted the American black revolt and civil rights struggles to being viewed in an isolated way, to being viewed simply as a continuation of American history, with no international connections.

This difference in perspective can be seen in Malcolm X's very early, and from the very beginning, unambiguous, quick and strong opposition to the white, racist, colonialist war in Vietnam and his support of the Vietnamese "rice eaters," fighting against white American military power, even before Vietnam had become the trauma and political issue it eventually became. On the other hand, while King, after the assassination of Malcolm X, eventually came out against the war in Vietnam--and this is to his credit--it was a tortuous decision which he was dragged into because Vietnam became more and more the overwhelming American issue. King's timid opposition seemed to be dependent more on balancing and weighing what the responses would be, and what would return him to the spotlight than any real political principle or comprehension. Even so, King's opposition to the Vietnam war cost him the support of many, Negroes and whites. By contrast, because of his clear anti-colonialism stance, Malcolm X's DESIRE FOR AMERICA'S MILITARY DEFEAT IN VIETNAM never lost him any support from his supporters and admirers.

With this preface, we can answer the previous question: The Americans were checked from using the excessive violence against the black revolt as witnessed e.g. against the African liberation movements or the Asian liberation movements like Vietnam because the USA was in a different objective position than these other white powers. I don't mean by this that there's a Constitution. The whites had trampled on and held no respect for the Constitution for decades when it came to black rights.

Nor do I mean that the Americans had some moral qualms against using violence against freedom fighters. This was being disproven by the Vietnam War. As a matter of fact, the USA has NEVER supported any anti-colonial movement by non-white peoples. Just the contrary: They have supported in weapons, money, logistics, intelligence, military personnel and soldiers the killings and massacres by all the white European oppressors of black and non-white peoples.

So what was it that checked white American power, a power which had previously exterminated millions of Native Americans, and was involved in the extermination of tens of millions of Africans in the slave trade? What caused them, instead of gunning down the black demonstrators, to opt to pay to control this revolt? To choose Martin King for this?

The answer to this question is part of understanding this international perspective which is a necessary part to understanding The True Meaning of Malcolm X.

Part 5[5]

In Part 4, I have continued the analysis that to understand what Malcolm X was about it is absolutely necessary to place him in his right political reference frame, or coordinates. This was black nationalism. Something not at all espoused, indeed, was spoken against by Martin King and the Negro civil rights leaders, all of whom were, most relevantly, distinguished from Malcolm X by the fact they were all being paid for by the blacks' enemies, the white power structure. Malcolm X was not.

Malcolm X's black nationalist perspective made him take as the field of his action the international arena versus the purely national or American perspective of Martin King. That this international perspective seemed most naturally from a black nationalist position can be seen with that other great black nationalist leader of this century, Marcus Garvey, whose program for the liberation of blacks 50 years earlier to Malcolm was entirely international. And before Garvey, last century, Martin Delany. All of whom held that blacks in America must identify themselves as Africans, with African liberation as an important part of their platform. But these discussions we can't enter into here.

Malcolm X identified and saw as the African American allies all the non-white peoples in the world struggling against white oppression. As an example of this focus, Malcolm X frequently made allusions to the Bandung Conference of 1954. The Bandung Conference was a gathering by all non-white peoples from around the globe to discuss the questions and strategies of their liberations. They kept the white man out, and they began to see that they all faced common problems and a common enemy. To wit: the white man's oppressive and exploitative system.

The question the reader was left with was the question why is it that racist America did not respond to African Americans in their revolts like the whites, e.g. in South Africa responded to the protests of their blacks? Why didn't the whites just gun the blacks down? The myth which has been offered is that the whites were overwhelmed by the higher moral efforts, magnetism and appeals of Martin King, who was America's answer to Gandhi.

In truth, the answer is dramatically different, and it is just in this international field where this truth is to be found. This truth is something the

King followers want no part of since they've been paid to support a completely bogus myth, viz. the King myth. They've been paid billions to foster a purely American protest movement, where the barriers supposedly fell before the moral, non-violent protests of Martin King.

That King's non-violent successes were entirely based on this international situation in which the USA found itself, and represented a gutting of the black revolution are matters which no official histories, books or commentators dare suggest. Nor the fact that King wasn't even necessary for these successes, unlike with Malcolm X for the success of the black revolution. If there were no King, this level of success was assured because there were many others vying to be the top leader, the movement couldn't be stopped, and the whites were paying. King's position came in virtue of the whites choosing and banking on him. Unlike what happened to Malcolm X after his death, after King's assassination, King's followers continued and the civil rights movement chalked up even more and greater gains.

This is an example of what I meant in the second article of this series when I stated "there's No Such Thing as an 'objective history.'" The official histories and accounts may offer true film clippings and reports of demonstrations and legislations passed. But they have "selected (in and out) and interpreted" these documents to prove their case. One can prove almost anything by careful selecting, editing and interpreting the documents, even without all the lies, distortions and deceit which always accompany such "histories." Voltaire once cleverly remarked, "History is just those tricks we play on the dead."

I also mentioned in that second article when defining "nominally objective," that in what I present about Malcolm X--my selection and interpretation processes--no new facts or information can ever be presented which would materially alter what I have to present as the true meaning of Malcolm X. Further to this, I stated, in all other interpretations and selections, this would not be the case. The King forces' selections and interpretations are destroyed when this international situation is brought to bear.

However, to be sure of ourselves, it should be clear to everyone except to the truly historically and politically ignorant and naive, the white man simply could not have been that impressed either with Martin King, his demonstrations, his speeches, his person, his message, or his moral appeal. This is nuts! In the history of this long world, social and political power has never given in to such puffery, Mahatma Gandhi notwithstanding. The British, while certainly more impressed with Gandhi as a person than ever could be afforded Martin King, nevertheless, their relinquishing of India had little to do with being impressed with Gandhi's non-violence tactics. Naturally, this is not the space to argue such a point. Nevertheless, I should point out that Gandhi's Hindu principle of ahimsa (non-injury) was not all the principle--something which doesn't change--as has been proffered. As a matter of fact, Gandhi cut a deal with the British to use Indian forces in the British's very violent campaign against its enemy, Hitler. (Furthermore, Ghandhi was a lover of Krishna's Bhagavad-Gita, the most famous of Hindu texts, which argues FOR the use of violence in repelling evil.)

All of King's appeals, speeches, points of view, the whites had heard many times before. Nor did King invent the non-violent protests used by blacks. And I've indicated the American whites' past, and then present. Therefore, common logic alone demands another explanation.

For the record, here was Malcolm X's understanding before his split from the Nation of Islam: Malcolm X believed what Elijah Muhammad had told him. Namely, that the white man was an evil invention by a mad black scientist named Yakub, who, experimenting with skin graftings and biology, in a Dr. Frankenstein sort of fashion, created this moral monster, who was a devil: the white man. That the white man had been given 6,000 years to rule by Allah. Now, having had full reign to his madness, where he had raped, plundered, massacred and exterminated countless millions of non-white peoples, the white man's 6,000 years were drawing to a close. His time was up. The rise of non-white peoples was sponsored by divine fiat. The white man's ruin was imminent. The blacks' time for liberation was at hand.

I'll call this belief the Yakub fable. Lest one thinks less of Malcolm X or wishes to patronize his intelligence for swallowing such a fable, it should be pointed out--to many unsuspecting readers' shock--that many intelligent and educated people today still believe in such fables as Adam and Eve and talking serpents; of Noah's Ark and whatnot.

These are fables, not truth, not history. People's sole reason for believing in these fables is because some spiritual authority said this was true, information which claims to come from God. Elijah Muhammad was Malcolm's spiritual authority, and Muhammad claimed to have received this Yakub knowledge directly from Allah, who appeared to Elijah in Person.

At that time, I was a Marxist and atheist of a black nationalist bent, and although I was just a teenager I was respected as a young theoretician by my political mentor and some others. (E. g. at 18, after Malcolm's assassination, I self-published my first book. Using the theoretical tool of Marx's historical materialist dialectics, I analyzed and explained the history and meaning of Chinese philosophy and sages from Confucius to Mao Tse-tung.) Here is what I and many black nationalists and some radicals believed at that time:

After World War II, the Americans became the de facto rulers and leaders of the non-communist white, capitalist worlds. The white worlds were built since Columbus on the murder, extermination, enslavement, land grab, colonization and exploitation of the raw goods, materials and labor of blacks and other non-white peoples. This was the material basis for the development of the modern Western, capitalist world.

The major wars of this century involving America, World Wars I, II, Korea, and Vietnam were capitalist and colonialist wars. World War I was at its seat a squabble by various European powers over the spoils of African and Third World colonizations. Since countries like Germany developed late, and given that the Western world was built on and sustained by having people to exploit, but because the favorable territories were already spoken for, the same logic prevailed upon the European powers as amongst upstart gangsters who fought the established bosses over territories to sell their bootlegged liquor. Indeed, Lenin saw all the capitalist countries in exactly that description:

World War II was a continuation of WW I, as agreed by all. In this case, Hitler attempted to break the stranglehold the allies had dealt Germany in the first World War. Japan changed sides in this War and was active in grabbing territories of the Far East, including taking Vietnam (Indochina) from the French. The reason, in fact, Japan bombed Pearl Harbor had to do with securing its Pacific oil supplies, which U.S. was continually threatening.

The results of WW II were such that the European colonial powers were broken. Only the United States stood in the path of the international communist onslaught. No other world power could stop this communist thrust. The great albatross for America was the fact that the communists' great appeal to the Third World was the fact that their history was clean of racist and colonial oppression; whereas, America and the European powers were clearly the guilty parties. The enemies of non-whites. Within this context, it was the communist forces which supported all the African, Asian, Latin American and global struggles against the European and American white powers.

The one chance the West had, in the powerfully important War of Propaganda, was to convince the Third World that America actually represented for them liberty and freedom, whereas the communists represented oppression and political slavery. But there rang a loud hollowness in this. The first African country to gain its Independence, Ghana in 1954 was led by Nkrumah a Marxist. Around the world, Marxist and anti-colonialist styled revolutions were taking hold. The greatest fear, because of its closeness to the United States, was the Cuban revolution which turned Marxist. But throughout the world, in jungles around the globe, there were these real life and death struggles over capitalism versus communism. The trip wire in all of these wars was the anti-colonialist and anti-racist struggles being waged by non-white peoples. Most of the world is non-white, and their resources are needed to run and maintain the West's economic engines, life support systems and standards of living.

For the United States to fire on the blacks, given her special role in this international struggle, meant to lose EVERYTHING. It meant losing the Propaganda War. It meant that the black revolt, which couldn't be stopped, ran the risk of becoming a mass movement susceptible to communist influence and takeover. It risked pushing America over the brink, with civil war breaking out, where the international communist movement would take a strong seat, clutching inside the belly of the beast a long knife which would cut out from the inside America's heart and capacity. America would have a "fifth column" and be forced to wage a two front war against the communists to a much greater, galactic extent than was the case. This at a time when America and European colonialists appeared to be losing anyway. Consequences could be America lost all pretences to being a democratic society, as open repression and political murder became the rule, leading possibly to a fascist dictatorship or communist victory.

This is why Martin King was used and paid to control and channel the black revolution into the Negro revolution. This was the white man's fear. All this King nonsense when viewed by these facts exposes the King myth for what it is: something paid for by blacks' oppressors and given to ignorant people all too ready to be bought off.

Understanding this Marxist analysis, (I'm presently no longer a Marxist and haven't been one for nearly 20 years, and I will present a third analysis in the following article), and seeing how the Yakub fable which projected the end of white rule converged with the Marxist theory which projected the end of capitalist rule are major clues to understanding why he was gunned down and The True Meaning of Malcolm X.

PART 6[6]

In the last article I showed how the black nationalism of Malcolm X placed his conception of the African American struggle within the context of a worldwide struggle being waged by all non-whites, which differed significantly from King and the Negro leaders who even today portray the struggles during the sixties as solely an American struggle, and how this positively impacted and underwrote the blacks' struggle in America. Everything has been put into supporting a national myth. The myth of King.

Because of this failure, there's a lack of real comprehension that the black revolt contained at least two struggles being fought in America. One was the more obvious struggle against laws permitting segregation and discrimination against African Americans, the struggle which included but went far beyond the struggle King represented. This second struggle was a fight for true black liberation because it directly related to blacks' economic and political freedom from whites, and this struggle was represented by Malcolm X.

The first struggle confronted two different white American power groups in opposition to each other because of their respective different interests. This white power versus white power conflict was on the surface and out in the open, because it was one group of whites who was paying King and the Negro leaders to fight the other white group. This opposition between the two white powers was symbolized best during the sixties when Governor George Wallace stood in the doorway of the state's university to block Kennedy's court orders to desegregate. But there had been a series of other confrontations beginning with the Supreme Court decision in 1954 to desegregate public schools. The fifties saw Eisenhower call out federal troops to Little Rock, Arkansas.

This conflict between the two white power structures was in a mini way a reprise of the conflict between the interests of the same two white power groups in the American Civil War. In the last century a conflict between the Northern "Big Boys'" interests, representing manufacturing and financed capital versus the smaller and more limited Southern, plantation capital's interests. The black slaves were the center of this conflict of interests. The Northern "Big Boys" had no need of slave labor, and, indeed, saw this anachronism as an impediment to industrial and more and more technological capitalism. The Civil War resulted. It never was "a moral issue." It was a Capital issue.

The Northern "Big Boys," whose political figureheads were the radical Republicans defeated the South, freed the slaves, installed blacks into power, and protected them with federal troops. Constitutional Amendments and other laws were passed to assure blacks their rights and legal incorporation into American society. This eleven year period has been called "Black Reconstruction."

Then blacks were betrayed in 1877 by this same Northern power group once they got what they really wanted (like, "thank you ma'am"): the free flow of capital on the basis of free, not slave labor. The military protection to blacks was withdrawn, and the deal reached with the Southern power was that the Northern "Big Boys" would no longer interfere with the South and would renege on their commitment to support Constitutional rights for blacks. The Southern white power structures were free, under the banner of "States' rights," to deal with "their niggers" as they saw fit. The agreement was there'd be no interference from this bigger Northern white power in the South's campaigns and laws of terrorism, political defanging, humiliation and de facto economic re-enslavement of blacks.

But because of this new international situation, the Northern "Big Boys" had new interests. They, in turn, according to these interests, had to renege on their previous agreement with the Southern white powers. (Depending as their interests shifted, they double-crossed both sides, blacks and whites.) The Northern "Big Boys'" interests concerned international capital and the newest technologies, global power, foreign countries, market places, world class military power, life and death struggles eventually implicating every person on this planet. These struggles came home in focus up close with the Cuban Missile Crisis. Here the several dimensions of Third World, anti-colonialism and anti-imperialism, communist revolution, the shores of America, internal radical political formations and oppositions, American military power and nuclear holocaust all converged.

By comparison, the Southern white power interests in oppressing blacks were, at bottom, uneconomic or only marginally economic. Their demands were parochial, mean-spirited, and just egotistical: a need to feel superior and have society support this superiority feeling by having the legal and social right to treat black folks like human dogs! This Northern "Big Boys'" interest therefore turned against the Southern white power structures for reasons given. While every tale and theory have been advanced as to why President Kennedy was assassinated, one that hasn't been advanced, but which was undoubtedly an added reason, is a reprise of the South's reason for the assassination of Lincoln.

It was this same Southern white power that assassinated Martin King. But it was the Northern "Big Boys" who assassinated Malcolm X. Malcolm X was assassinated because of the second struggle being waged, since, on the surface, blacks in New York and the North already had many of the rights that King was struggling to give blacks in the South, like voting, eating in public facilities, sitting where they pleased on public busses, etc. Therefore, there had to be for a different reason, reflecting a different struggle, and by a different agent that Malcolm X was assassinated.

I indicated at the end of the previous article that I would provide a third point of view, differing both from Elijah Muhammad's Yakub fable believed in by Malcolm X, and the 400 year end to capitalism's theory advanced by various Marxists. In a sense, this view combines (the truthful) elements of both beliefs. The merit of this theory is that it's consistent with all the facts it purports to explain, something neither the Yakub fable nor Marxist theory can do.

This theory recognizes the truth of how various white powers since the appearance of Columbus exterminated, enslaved and exploited the lands, and raw materials of non-white peoples. This was the material basis for the development of the Western world. This analysis differs from the

Marxist view in that it states that this activity was designed and sponsored by the Divine Mind (God). The Marxists are atheists, and in their eyes this development was simply the appearance and development of capitalism.

On the other hand, various blacks who also accept these facts but believe in the Divine Mind are at a loss to explain the two together. It's that old problem that if there's a God, how can evil exist in the world? Some religions have created the idea of a devil or evil source. But this doesn't really answer the question, since the question still remains, transposed to how can a devil exist? Further responses are attempted.

The answer is really that the Divine Mind while itself is the Good allows evil to exist in the material world. I do not have the space to elaborate on this, but I should remark that the Bibe has God saying, "I create good and evil." The Divine Mind works through history. Marx, who was a philosopher, believed that nature created by destroying what came before it. However one wants to see it, as white devils or a murderous capitalism, the European powers' role was destruction of all the old social orders, in order to lay the basis for new human ages and societies.

This rampage and destruction, horrors and terrors continued for nearly 400 years, which engulfed all non-white peoples and their lands. Many social formations were wiped out. Africans in addition to dying by the tens of millions in the slave trade, and enduring slavery on a larger and more brutal scale than slavery ever before, suffered their lands to be invaded and colonized by whites. This was all the Divine Mind's Will. This was the Divine Mind's way of tearing down the old as the necessary preludes to building something new: new human ages and human possibilities.

However, something changed with the Twentieth Century. The Divine Mind decided to call a halt to the white man's rampage and rule.

Understanding that the Divine Mind had given the whites 400 years to be destructive and exploitative against blacks and other non-whites, but the Twentieth Century would see an unrolling of their political rule over non-whites, because the whites had accomplished the destructive tasks assigned to them, forms the background theory to understanding the major political and military events of this century. These major political and military events of the Twentieth Century, in turn, with this background theory, explain the appearance and The True Meaning of Malcolm X.

PART 7[7]

In the previous article I pointed out that there were in fact two struggles being waged by blacks, one, the more limited one, which consisted of desegregating the South and which became symbolized by Martin King. This struggle was the Negro revolution. The second struggle, represented by Malcolm X, aimed for economic and political freedom from whites. This was the black revolution. The implications of this second struggle is what caused Malcolm X's assassins to be a different white power group, the Northern "Big Boys," than the Southern white power group which assassinated King, although for certain this Southern white power structure could only fear and hate Malcolm X worse than King. But King had the support and was in the pay of Malcolm's assassins.

I also began a third conceptual framework to view events, which differed both from the Yakub fable created by Elijah Muhammad and believed by Malcolm X, or the Marxist theory, which I at that time myself believed, and which was held by many serious political thinkers and activists. This theory presents the notion that the Divine Mind was the real Mover and ultimate Agent for the destruction wrought by whites against blacks and other non-whites. That the purpose was to brutally destroy and uproot older societies for the purpose of laying the foundation so newer human ages with newer human possibilities could grow and be built. The atheist Marxists held this to be true as well, but they didn't believe in God. The black and non-white victims, while for the most part believing in God, could never bear to face or admit the sure logic such a belief entailed.

I left matters by stating that this white onslaught had been given a period of 400 years, but the Twentieth Century was the time that the Divine Mind had decided would see a halt and rollback to the white man's power and oppression of non-whites around the world. That the whites had achieved the purpose for which they'd been given divine power to effect.

One might question why should one believe in a Divine Mind in this history? There are many reasons, including philosophical and factual reasons. But one of the more impressive reasons is prophecies, some projected hundreds of years into the future. I don't mean the vaguenesses and disputations involving Bible prophecies. I mean people like Nostradamus (1503-1566) who continues to astound people by his predictions of specific events occuring hundreds of years after his death. In some cases he's even predicted specific events in specific years. But there have been others, including prophets and seers among the very people conquered by the whites. Jomo Kenyatta in his classic, "Facing Mount Kenya," reports on a prophet of his tribe, the Kikuyus, who predicted years in advance the appearance of the white man, and stated details of some things the whites would do, like building a railroad, unknown and not understood by the tribesmen.

Thus, these three points of view all agree that something was ending for the white man. The Yakub fable held that Allah would finally obliterate the white devils from the planet in an Armaggedon styled finish of good against evil. The Marxists whose theoretical eyes only saw economic systems held that the working class would finally obliterate the devilish capitalist system from the planet in an Armaggedon styled social and political revolution of good against evil. But I maintain that the Divine Mind chose only to end the yoke of racist and capitalist oppression by whites against the non-whites, which is in keeping with the facts thus far. To speculate what more this entails is not in keeping with our intent in writing these series of articles on The True Meaning of Malcolm X.

Previously, in article 5, we gave the Marxist interpretation of World Wars I and II, Korea and Vietnam, the major wars of the Twentieth Century as they related to America. I will not here repeat what was stated there. Rather I must add to the interpretation in light of this third point of view being offered.

The deeper meaning of WW I was actually to create the conditions to bring to birth the success of Lenin's Russian Revolution, a communist revolution which was IMPOSSIBLE without that War. The reason the Divine Mind chose this white communist power's birth on the world stage was to later aid and assist the non-whites to obtain their liberation from the yoke of the white capitalist powers. The non-whites were simply unable on their own to gain their freedom from colonial and racist rules without another military and political power to help them.

Remember, blacks gained their freedom from slavery in America because they had the military support and backing of the North. The North's real interest in freeing the slaves was not morality or hating the pains and sufferings of the blacks. They had dollars and cents interest in a different economic system, a capitalism of wage labor. Because of this Northern power, a conflict and war precipitated in which blacks were the beneficiaries. Conversely, as I've indicated, when the blacks lost this Northern white power support, they were betrayed to terrible enemy who reveled in treating blacks like human dogs.

If the Divine Mind, after four centuries of building whites up to awesome levels of power, power invested in knowledge and intelligence, the military, institutions and networks, economies supporting millions, and tremendous amounts of money, how in the blazes could these non-whites defeat the whites when these non-whites existed still on a much lower platform in all these areas of power? This could be accomplished if because of seriously different interests another white power came forth to support these non-white peoples struggling for their freedoms. This is exactly the role the communists have played this century.

But the Russians were not by themselves capable of fighting all of the strong European capitalist powers. Therefore, WW II was necessary to bring forth Hitler, whose job was to break the legs of the European colonial powers. This is exactly what Hitler did. Because of Hitler's devastations on Britain and France as examples, post WW II was the emergence of the non-white independence movements. The momentum began with India in 1947, then China in 1949 and it just steamrollered from country to country and from continent to continent.

This is how the white racist Americans found themselves fighting the Vietnamese War. The French had been broken by Hitler and so could no longer defend their colonial acquisitions. The Japanese took over the French's claims in

Indochina. After the War, the French believed they could return to their rape and plunder. But because the Divine Mind said otherwise, the French were defeated in this effort, most notably in 1954, and called upon the US for help. They received this US help, and the Americans lied then, and have not stopped lying about their reasons for being in Southeast Asia, or the fact that they truly lost the Vietnam War, despite fighting as hard as they could. The US dropped more bombs on Vietnam than had been dropped by all sides during WW II. Or, in the history of mankind and wars.

Vietnam, as Malcolm X understood it, was a racist and imperialist war. Most importantly, since the US was the world's greatest white racist military power, their defeat there meant definitively that the whites no longer had the divine power to oppress non-white peoples in ways they had known to do previously. Moreover, THE U.S.'S MILITARY DEFEAT IN VIETNAM HASTENED AND ASSURED THE SUCCESS OF THE NEGRO REVOLUTION IN AMERICA. Not King.

It's important to point out, as an adjunct to the above, that the US's claim to be fighting communism, while true, nevertheless, fails to explain why they fought so hard against communism? What was so terrible about communism? The whites claimed that the communists suppressed freedom. So what the hell were racism, colonialism and imperialism, libertinism??!! The suppressed facts expose this: Ho Chi Ming and every revolutionary movement, just as Nelson Mandela pointed out about his African Nationalist Congress, had first asked, begged, pleaded with America to help them gain their liberation against white, oppressive colonialist rule. Practically every freedom group by non-whites around the world requested this aid. The Americans NEVER aided the non-white struggle against the European powers. Not one! So there's a clear lie to the claim the US was fighting the communists for the Vietnamese's freedom.

So, Ho Chi Ming, like the African freedom fighters turned to the Russian and Chinese communists for support. Without this communist support, which the Divine Mind placed for the benefit of non-white peoples (and communism's collapse can be viewed as "mission accomplished" with no further purpose for communism's existence), the political maps at the end of the Twentieth Century would look little different in substance from the way the political maps looked at the start of the Twentieth Century. At the beginning of this century, within the lifetime of many still living today, the white man from different white nations ruled and had economically colonized either directly or indirectly the entire non-white worlds. Such control supported a system of beliefs concerning white superiority which made a non-white a despised creature even in his own land. And at the very bottom of those despised were the blacks.

It was this larger context of battle that Malcolm X, as I've asserted, was entering and leading African Americans with his black nationalist program for black liberation. And it was this fear of Malcolm's entry by the Northern "Big

Boys'" white power group that led them to murder Malcolm X.

Nevertheless, this white power structure had ready black allies in the killing of Malcolm X, most notably the Black Muslims, members of whom stalked Malcolm X, and at least one of Malcolm's confessed assassins claims to have been a member of the Nation of Islam. In many ways, Elijah Muhammad and the Nation of Islam bear much greater responsibility for the murder of Malcolm X than do the CIA and other agencies which duped and/or paid several of the black assassins. I must close this part of the circle before there is complete understanding concerning Malcolm's assassination.

To do so, in the next article I must return to the issue of Malcolm X's commitment to black liberation, a subject I first raised in article 3, and I must explain the statement I made then that this commitment by Malcolm X forced his enmity with Elijah Muhammad and the Nation of Islam, which eventually forced him out. Following Malcolm's ouster, objectively, and probably also consciously, the Black Muslims joined forces with the CIA, FBI and other white agencies in the assassination of Malcolm X.

The tying together these more focussed on areas is important for a fuller appreciation of The True Meaning of Malcolm X.

PART 8[8]

In the previous article I gave the outline to a third theory, differing both from what Malcolm X believed, and what I as a political activist and theorist believed at the time. This theory, in brief, sees the Divine Mind (God) as active in history, using whites and the stages of capitalist development to uproot and destroy older anthropological and historical developments, many having existed for many thousands of years, for the purpose of laying the foundation for new human ages. That this campaign of extermination, enslavement and exploitation had been given 400 years, but the Twentieth Century saw a change and that the Divine Mind precipitated major wars and events for the expressed purpose of liberating the non-white worlds from whites. This is the meaning of the Russian Revolution which brought the communists to power, since their purpose was to provide the needed support to non-whites struggling against the American and European racist powers.

To be sure, the communists who officially never believed in God never saw this as their real purpose. Nor did Hitler, the racist fascist, who believed he was following God's plans, understand that his role was to break the legs of the European colonial powers, after which the rush was on by non-whites around the world to liberate themselves. Blacks in America made their progress in this same rush and worldwide momenta. The Vietnam War was the final proof that a white racist military power did not have the Divine Mind's support to recolonize a non-white people. The military defeat of the US war machine was greatly beneficial to blacks' struggles in America. The blacks' struggles and victories became easier and more assured with America's loss.

Further to this, I've pointed out the fact that Malcolm X's black revolution incorporated but went far beyond King's Negro revolution, which explains both why King received the Northern "Big Boys'" white pay and support against the Southern white power structures, but why this same white Northern "Big Boys" assassinated Malcolm X. Before I detail a few of the significant differences between King's Negro revolution, which has resulted ultimately in all the ills facing blacks today and the devastating black social statistics after all of King's ostensible goals and advocated legal changes having been won, facts which the present Negro leaders, the heirs to King, wish to avoid discussing at all cost, versus Malcolm X's black revolution, I must close the circle because it still were the blacks, most particularly, members of the Nation of Islam which fomented hatred, made death threats, and finally, participated in the murder of Malcolm X.

This calls up the question, why was Malcolm X kicked out of the Black Muslim movement? As an example of the trivialization and shallowness laid on this important issue, an example of a side show and something not very significant in the scheme of things becoming the main event, the sexual misconduct of Elijah Muhammad with his teenaged secretaries whom he impregnated and then kicked out of the organization has been cited as the reason for the split. This type of "talk show" or soap level of voyeurism is a sure-fire way of perking ignorant and lazy-minded people's interest, because for such people it's too boring and difficult to think above such a level. Sex sells. And illicit sex sells even more. But the plain truth of the matter is that the weight of significance of Malcolm X and the then Nation of Islam, the fate of millions of blacks did not and could not have turned on whatever "dirty old man" weaknesses that Elijah Muhammad suffered from. This is nuts!

True, Malcolm X did make this allegation against Elijah Muhammad, and this allegation was stated to be the reason at least one of the Black Muslim assassins stated was his motive for participating in Malcolm's assassination. But the plain facts will show that Malcolm's public allegation came AFTER his ouster from the Nation of Islam, AFTER many months of the Black Muslims ceaselessly and continuously in print and speeches castigating and excoriating Malcolm X, who publicly stated he only wanted peace with the Black Muslims and gave nothing but respect and praise to Elijah Muhammad, and AFTER many death threats and attempts on Malcolm's life by the Black Muslims.

Nor was this knowledge of Elijah Muhammad's shameless role with these girls what precipitated his leaving the Nation. Ostensibly, the break came when Malcolm X was silenced by Elijah Muhammad for 90 days because of Malcolm's forbidden statement that Kennedy's assassination was a case of "the chickens coming home to roost." Malcolm X was 100% and totally submissive and accepting of this censure by Elijah Muhammad, 100% and totally accepting that he had erred, 100% and totally blamed himself for his indiscretion, 100% and totally confirmed that Elijah

Muhammad was Malcolm's leader and he was following Elijah. These statements at the time hardly suggest that Malcolm X was in a combative or splitting mode with Elijah Muhammad over Elijah's sexual misconduct.

As a matter of fact, Malcolm X was 100% and totally committed to returning to his position in the Nation of Islam after the 90 day suspension. He remained silent and refused to speak during those 90 days. But after the 90 days, it's just that Malcolm X was not allowed back. Malcolm X had been kicked out of the Black Muslims without even the courtesy to tell him so. Malcolm X, like all mortals, had to make a living. He had to do something. He could not remain silent forever. Malcolm X had to accept the fait accompli. So Malcolm X publicly stated that he was now on his own, and was going to form two different organizations. One strictly religious, the Muslim Mosque, Inc., and another, a much broader black nationalist organization to include blacks of all or no religious persuasion, the Organization of African American Unity (OAAU).

It is in the formation of this second organization, the OAAU, and Malcolm's irreverent remarks about Kennedy's assassination which we must see as forming the pieces for the true reason for Malcolm's ouster from the Black Muslim movement. Because, as stated, after Malcolm's split with Elijah, after Malcolm X gave his praises and respects to Elijah and begged for peace between them as he went on his separate course, the Nation of Islam, nevertheless, physically dogged and threatened Malcolm X and continued to attack him in print and from podiums. Why didn't they just let Malcolm X be? If Malcolm had strayed from the teachings, just leave him be. Why were they so insistent on killing Malcolm X?

I know. I was there. The last time I saw Malcolm X was in a speech he gave in Detroit, one week before his assassination, and the day his home in New York had been fire bombed. Outrageously, the Muslims claimed Malcolm bombed his own home!! I met Malcolm again after this speech in his hotel room. I served as an unarmed bodyguard. I remember there were about 50 Black Muslims who had showed up at Malcolm's speech, intimidating the crowd. I remember thinking for certain that I was going to be killed, but I never had a second of reservation when asked to take this position. In fact, it's somewhat embarrassing now for Malcolm to say so--but I now recognize the Divine element in this, although at that time as I've written I neither believed in God nor life after death--but I was the ONLY one who agreed to serve as a bodyguard for Malcolm X on this day, Sunday, February 14, 1965, so threatening were these mean looking and very serious Black Muslim soldiers. The ONLY one.

So the annoying question persists: why didn't the Black Muslims, after Malcolm X had left and wanted to make his break on friendly terms, just let Malcolm X be? There were a plethora of black leaders outside of the Nation of Islam, and Malcolm X would just be another one of these. Why did Farrakhan and company continue to hound and dog and eventually join forces with the white Northern "Big Boys" to gun down Malcolm X? One has to be OUT OF HIS MIND (or, just plainly stupid) to believe these things had anything WHATSOEVER to do with Elijah Muhammad screwing his teenaged secretaries.

The answer to these questions and how the OAAU and the Kennedy remark fit into the puzzle returns us to the personal commitment Malcolm X had to the liberation of black people. I've previously indicated that ONLY Malcolm X of all the prominent national black leaders was 100% committed to the liberation of blacks. Others were less committed, being compromised in their commitments by their fears of physical violence from whites, by their creature comforts, by the money they could either make or lose, by their career goals, etc. Not committed 100% to the liberation of blacks. All the Negro leaders were seeking big cash from whites. Malcolm X was the only national black leader not being paid for by whites.

This major difference between Malcolm X and all the other leaders, and in particular, Martin King cannot be slighted in importance. Only by having an independent financial base can blacks ever expect to be 100% committed to black liberation. It is simply IMPOSSIBLE to be committed to black liberation, while being paid for and needing funding from whites. The black church became the vehicle for blacks funding local church leaders, which explains why so many of the civil rights leaders were ministers. It's not simply because of some leadership capacity and references to God. Whites' political leaders aren't ministers, nor were the African, Asian or Latin American revolutions led by ministers. Rather, ministers had an economic base which had sufficient freedom to stop the whites from taking away their economic livelihoods when they opposed whites. Conversely, it's always been the strategy of whites, for this very reason, to keep the blacks financially dependent on them.

Malcolm X's sincerity caused him to attack all the Negro leaders who were betraying the black revolution for their own personal comforts. They were selling the struggle out. He directly accused King of selling out. Eventually, Malcolm's commitment to real black liberation struck home the phoniness of the Nation of Islam which consequently forced him out.

Why was Malcolm forced out? Because Elijah Muhammad proved to be in the final analysis just like so many of the other Negro preachers. On a different level, for sure. Further up the pyramid of commitment to black liberation than others, to be sure. But still, Elijah Muhammad was satisfied with all the money that was pouring in each month from his followers, the women, the limosines, his pedestaled "prophet" status, his creature comforts. He didn't want to battle or fight the white man. Malcolm X was carrying matters too far. He was bringing down too much heat on them. With that Kennedy remark, enough was enough. Malcolm X had to go.

Elijah's position that blacks should not seek integration nor civil rights but hold out for a return by blacks to Africa or until whites gave several States to blacks allowed the Black Muslims the comfort of talking tough without much doing, and no confrontations. It allowed Elijah the comfort of just hauling in millions from blacks with just a small percentage returned. Malcolm's forming new organizations was a direct financial threat to Elijah's cash flow. The officials in the Nation of Islam feared that Malcolm X, and not Elijah Muhammad, was the real cash drawing card, that many of Elijah's followers would abandon the Black Muslims for the Muslim Mosque, Inc. and the OAAU. That their ability to gain over more black members would be seriously undercut by Malcolm's existence.

Indeed, their fears were well based. It was Malcolm X who increased Elijah's membership after decades of Elijah's apostleship from around 400, mostly members, nationwide when Malcolm joined the Nation of Islam, to over 40,000 members and millions of supporters when Malcolm X left 12 years later, who put this unknown cult on the public map, and made the Nation of Islam known worldwide. Malcolm X, Elijah Muhammad, made the Nation of Islam!

Joining with the Nation of Islam was the Northern "Big Boys'" white power who also feared Malcolm's very strong, self-possessing power. A self-originating (as opposed to white created and paid) power to draw masses of blacks into his newly formed OAAU, which the white man knew was not for sale. A radical black organization which would link African Americans with struggling Africans, Arabs and other non-whites around the world, whose vast resources of lands, goods and materials, and peoples were the very matters being fought over by various interested parties.

This fear by members of the Nation of Islam of losing their cash flow from Malcolm's competing organizations fitted in nicely with the "Big Boys'" fear that Malcolm X might negatively impact the balance of World Power and their cash flow, which formed the basis for alliance. Behind the scenes and with black puppets and Black Muslim dupes, the white "Big Boys" were able to stop his placing the masses of blacks on the world stage, and to stop Malcolm X's very bold and spectacular bid for World Power!

The proof this was the Black Muslims' real motive in killing Malcolm is the de-emphasising of the political struggle after Malcolm's ouster; and after Elijah's death in 1975, his son successor began a systematic dismantling of all businesses the Nation of Islam had been identified with in the black communities. Eventually, even Farrakhan had to leave and form his own The New Nation of Islam in order to be more than just black mosques, which, like the black Christian churches, operate soley to give services and collect donations. Some, collecting many millions of dollars.

This is The True Meaning of Malcolm X.

PART 9[9]

In these last two articles, I want to touch on some of the differences between what Malcolm X was about versus what Martin King has proven to be about as they relate to the different political conceptualizations and agenda of the two. I've been explaining all along just how shallow and false the teachings and propaganda have been concerning the significance and dimensions of the African American struggle, and how the blacks' enemies, the whites have managed this common view not only by their control of all the media, but also by paying for the Negro leaders and their organizations which don't provide any different analyses or insights into the struggle than the white mass media. I believe I've proven my points thus far.

But there's much much more. Up to now I have not sought to detail important differences between the black nationalist program which Malcolm X was proposing in his new organization the OAAU (Organization of African American Unity) versus that of Martin King's program. Nor can I hope in the remaining two articles to even touch on, not to mention elaborate on the many, many important, hardly trivial, differences between Malcolm X and Martin King. I have detailed some of these more important differences in a book I hope to publish in 1995 on the thirtieth anniversary of the assassination of Malcolm X, entitled, "Forgotten Differences Between Malcolm X and Martin King."

I've made repeated references to two struggles being fought. One struggle became the triumphant Negro revolution, which was the revolution paid for by the white Northern "Big Boys" essentially against the white Southern power structures. This struggle centered on returning to blacks Constitutional rights which had previously already been won by blacks directly after the Civil

War, and the passing of three important Amendments to the Constitution: the 13th, 14th and 15th Amendments. These victories were lost to blacks most glaringly in the infamous sell out of blacks to these same white Southern powers by the white Northern "Big Boys," which resulted in the end to "Black Reconstruction," and the reappearance of white terrorist rule.

The second revolution was the black revolution, and in its implication something feared by the white Northern "Big Boys," but supported by Malcolm X, and his OAAU was to be the organizational mechanism for carrying out this black revolution. The fact that Malcolm's perspective and focus were international is contained in the OAAU's name itself, because it was directly patterned after the OAU or Organization of African Unity, which is a sort of African United Nations or African NATO. In fact, Malcolm's last year included not just a trip to Mecca as a religious rite required of all Muslims, but much more importantly, Malcolm was making contacts with non-white world leaders throughout Africa and the oil rich Middle East.

I have established this first difference of international versus national outlook between Malcolm X and Martin King as a consequence of Malcolm's black nationalist perspective. But what is black nationalism as Malcolm X and before him, Marcus Garvey defined it?

The word "nation" is contained in nationalism. It required that blacks see themselves as a separate nation. But a nation had to have land in order to exist. So, black nationalism as all nationalism is a demand for land. Thus, Elijah Muhammad's Nation of Islam was a black nationalist movement, demanding separatism and land. Indeed, Elijah had previously been a follower of Marcus Garvey. But Malcolm X's connection to Garvey came more directly than through Elijah because Malcolm's minister father, who had been an active Garveyist, was murdered by klansmen. Elijah Muhammad only re-kindled a bitter and suppressed memory in Malcolm, whose father was murdered while he was still a little boy. Probably a lot of Malcolm's strong resentment to whites had its roots in this fact.

But Malcolm X went beyond this in his theoretical work, and I don't have space to elaborate on how Malcolm X was the theoretical fashioner who made plausible or at least defendable much of Elijah Muhammad's rather ignorant comprehension of history and the larger world. Like many other black prophets, swamis, exotics, yes, even God! (Father Divine), Elijah Poole had constructed his own fables to install himself amongst ignorant blacks, and thereby earn a very good living. But his ignorant fables were never thought to really venture outside the ignorant black communities, where anything bizarre and fantastic had still a good chance of making it.

Malcolm's great but untutored mind theorized, on his own, about all human conflicts, revolutions and wars in the history of the world. He concluded, in a flash of insight, that all revolutions were a struggle over land. This is very meaningful when one looks at all the wars being fought today around the world: how it's a struggle for the land.

But Malcolm X had come to realize that his black nationalism for African Americans had to be more active like Garvey's black nationalism and less like Elijah's. For this, the true essence of his black nationalism as it was for Garvey's, and which distingished itself from King was just this: black nationalism meant black independence vs. King's integration which meant black dependency. The many social ills affecting the black communities today, and which I've stated trace themselves to King, his program and legacy, as enforced and interpreted by all the Negro leaders, are the results of King's program of black dependency on whites!

The principle of independence was the real economic, political and cultural principle riveting and driving the worldwide non-white peoples' struggles. Independence. Black independence. Third World Independence. The anti-colonial movements were independence movements, just like the American Revolution against British colonialism had been. So too was the black revolution, an independence movement, which by definition could only take a black nationalist form.

In any question of independence, economic survival is foremost. Thus, the foremost element and heart of any independence movement in general and a black independence movement in particular must address itself to being economically and financially independent of one's former oppressor. In fact, the American Revolution was fought principally because of the economic benefits the

American colonists saw in their replacing the British for themselves in manufacturing and agriculture which linked up to international trade and commerce, and the colonists' meaning of freedom was economic freedom. This is why the Marxists call the American Revolution the revolution of the indigenous capitalist class (bourgeoisie).

Martin Delany, the father of American black nationalism, sought right after the Civil War to engage blacks in manufacturing and agriculture which would link up to international trade and commerce. He bought a ship for the trading segment. Marcus Garvey in the early part of this century, had similar ideas, and he too pruchased a ship to engage in international commerce. Malcolm X, the next point in this dangling and fallen line, had just begun to move in these economic directions, and his talk with non-white world leaders was a big step towards this end.

Hence, the black revolution directly addressed itself to black economic and financial independence from whites, while the Negro revolution was and is still imprisoned in a system of black economic and financial dependency on whites. But the black revolution incorporated the positive benefits of the Negro revolution like equal social and political treatment of blacks. But these gains would be made by blacks from a psoition of black economic independence, not begging dependency. Hence, Malcolm X after his split, had signalled that he too would join this phase of the blacks' struggle, something Elijah Muhammad had shunned.

One has a right to ask, why would the threat of blacks gaining their economic freedom from whites be so terrifying, enough so as to kill Malcolm X? It should be noted that upon the arrival of Marcus Garvey to America in the 1920's, J. Edgar Hoover, whose significance would later become known, wrote that his aim was to arrest Garvey, and he regretted that at present Garvey hadn't broken any laws. Not long afterwards, however, a black assassin fired several shots at Garvey, just grazing his target. The would-be black assassin was captured, and he threatened to expose who hired him. He was found hung in his cell the next day.

This fear and fight against blacks gaining their economic independence, even as this country had been touted as the unique place where (European) immigrants have come and gained theirs can only be explained by a deep-seated, psychological racist mentality possessed by whites. There were advantages to be gained by having a low class work force to do the menial work, particularly in the South, and the Marxists like presenting this economic motive as the sole reason. But there're economic advantages and disadvantages in any attitude one takes to a group of people. There's no especial reason to keep blacks as this menial class, since filling the ranks of the needy cuts across race.

When one looks at it, one finds the whites have hated or disdained all people, including other whites, who were different from themselves. The true meaning of America being the "great melting pot" has always referred--obviously--to the melting of other antagonistic white groups. The various white ethnic conflicts breaking out in Europe and the former Soviet Union recall former times in their respective histories. America offered the opportunity to submerge these killings and antagonisms amongst different white groups by their seeing the commonality of their skin color versus the skin color of non-whites. Without this skin color distinction being enforced, the various whites, who hated all others not like themselves, including other whites, could not "melt." The Jews in America have been the greatest beneficiaries of this. Among the non-whites, the blacks were unique in being a) the whites' color opposites, b) an 'integrated' member and contributor to white society (Native Americans, Mexicans, Chinese etc. were never 'integrated' members of white society, per se), and c) former slaves, and before then, "savages," and having a history of holding down the bottom of society.

This psychological need to maintain blacks as a reference point for hatred and for the bottom was a necessary part to allowing the "white melting pot" experiment to work, which in turn characterized the uniqueness of America. The major part of this resistance to black economic freedom, therefore, was purely racial psychology, not deeply economic, except in certain pockets. This is why J. Edgar Hoover, without this analysis, to be sure, wanted to see Garvey arrested if not killed. This is why Hoover later used his FBI to obstruct and fight against not only the black revolution, but King's Negro revolution was well. It had nothing deeper than a racist hatred of a group different than his, coupled with the false presumption that God ordained blacks should always be the servants of whites, placing into focus, much better than with animals, the higher status the white man represented among all of God's creations.

Next issue concludes this series on The True Meaning of Malcolm X.

PART 10[10]

There's much too much on this subject to compress in 10 articles. For the readers who had been following this series, they've received explosively new information and points of view. Information and points of view which have been suppressed in order to support a comprehension which the historic white enemies of blacks have paid for. Their view is the King myth, which has also been propagated by the paid for Negro leaders.

What I have done in these articles is to limit this awakening of the True Meaning of Malcolm X to three essential and interrelated points: 1) Establishing the criteria by which Malcolm X must be measured and understood, separating the wheat from various biographical chaff. This proves to be Malcolm's political vector of radical black nationalism, which differed fundamentally from King and the Negro leaders. 2) Malcolm's fundamental international perspective of the black struggle which proved to be the real basis for blacks' civil rights successes after WW II vs. King's purely national focus and comprehension. 3) Malcolm's principle of black independence, which meant foremost for Malcolm X black economic and financial independence vs. King's black dependency.

In this final article, I will address two points: i) what I previously defined as the whites' biggest Con Game, the violence vs. non-violence focus, snaring blacks into believing this is the issue separating Malcolm X from King, and ii) further elaboration of how the present terrible conditions facing many black communities are the results, consequences and exposed fallacies of King's principle and legacy.

It should now be clear that the fundamental issue separating Malcolm X from Martin King can be subsumed in point 3) above: Black independence vs. black dependence. Not violence vs. non-violence. Everything about Malcolm X flows from this distinction. A principle of black independence necessarily results in a principle of black nationalism, with its foremost component, black economic and financial independence, which naturally connects to an international trade and commerce position. It also means black independent politics. Nor can one be self-reliant economically and politically without believing in self-defense. This is where Malcolm X stood. Self-defense, while not peculiar to black nationalism, is nevertheless a necessary part of black nationalism.

The Big Lie and distortions have been to label Malcolm X's principle of black self-respect and self-defense as an advocacy of violence.

Malcolm never advocated violence. In fact, he was against violence. He wanted to end white violence through black self-defense. Let's be clear what this is about since the whites and their paid Negroes have distorted and lied so much about very recent history.

During and before Malcolm's time, whites felt they had the right to dress up in klansmen's uniforms and ride through the black communities, shooting, burning, raping, and, indeed lynching blacks at will. Blacks historically, long before King, practiced non-violence. Their non-violence was not due to any lofty Gandhi principle, but resulted from ranked, cold- hearted FEAR. Blacks were cowards in face of white terrorism, and whites wanted blacks to stay afraid of them. One black leader during the sixties, Robert F. Williams was chased out of the country because he advocated that blacks indeed had the CONSTITUTIONAL RIGHT to defend themselves against these klansmen night rides. Other black leaders who wanted to protect their communities received the greatest threats and pressures against them and their lives for telling blacks they had the right to self-defense.

King's position was that blacks should just suffer these terrorist murders by klansmen and other whites. Malcolm X opposed this as nonsense. Naturally, the whites were paying for King. Nevertheless, despite the propaganda, Malcolm X's position is followed today, not King's. You can be damned sure no klansmen are going to ride through any black community the way they previously did without expecting to be shot and killed by blacks. This is a tremendous change in attitude by blacks, and King had nothing to do with it. I don't have the space to expand on this self-defense principle and how it relates to other areas, but the truth is explained.

The second point is more pressing since today blacks have their greatest fear of being killed by other blacks--not klansmen. King's program is based on black dependency. What has resulted has been wholesale economic and financial abandonment of the black communities by blacks who've benefitted from the struggle.

To anybody who cares at all for logic, it's quite evident that the deteriorations of the black communities have come about since the rise and empowerment of blacks, the receding of the overt racism and exclusion of blacks. Therefore, it makes no logical sense whatsoever to ascribe these community failures to racism. It makes logical sense to ascribe these problems to the changes effected by the Negro leaders and their programs. These failures are the direct result of the blacks evading their financial obligations and investments in the black communities, passing this off to whites. How does this evasion translate into what we see today?

Any nation, society, group or family prospers in virtue that the material benefits are transferred--in different proportions--to the various members of that collective. When the leaders or upper classes of that group refuse to transfer or invest in any segment, then that uninvested segment deteriorates. It'd surprise no one if one farmer plowed, fertilized, seeded, watered, weeded, deinsected, etc. his field, and at season's end harvested a rich yield. While the field right next to this farmer, another farmer did nothing or next to nothing, and at season's end, this farmer had a weed and insect-infested field with a very poor and diseased yield. One isn't surprised because one knows this is a natural law.

Human economic and social laws are translations of these farmers' truths. The successful and stronger black members are supposed to invest their funds into the black communities--not the white communities. As blacks invest in the white communities, they build up the white communities and impoverish the black communities. The blacks have palmed off their investment responsibilities to whites. To the white government, white employers, white philanthropists. In turn, they've also transferred their authority to these anonymous whites. However, whites don't themselves have the same authority they previously had. Resentment of whites is open and fashionable. Therefore, there's a lack of authority in the black communities by anybody.

What compounds the situation than what previously existed is the very existence of successful and very successful blacks. The existence of blacks with incomes into the millions, tens of millions up to 100 million dollars a year. These facts affect other blacks who're both jealous of these other blacks, plus feel a loss of self-worth since these blacks are abandoned, and they can't too easily now believe only whites can succeed. This explains the patholgoical need for "respect," and material items. There is a serious ego problem.

The murders are means of gaining "respect." They're also easy to accomplish. What takes over is ability to succeed in anything which feeds this sociopathological ego. There are other components to this witch's brew, nearly all of which existed previously but the new dynamics have exacerbated the psychological soil in a way only big money and success on the one hand, and abandonment on the other hand, can.

The Negro leaders continue in their madness, in their persistence that not themselves but whites must take the financial risk and invest in blacks, that blacks have no fiancial responsibilities to blacks. They've managed to deceive the masses into believing the problem has been not them and their morally failed and shameful program of black financial abandonment and dependency but the Reagan-Bush's 12 years of government programs' slashes. But these slashes they've been screaming so loudly about are themselves proof of the stupidity of these Negro leaders' program. Unfortunately, the propaganda has been so one-sided that common sense can't even be heard. But this stupidity amongst blacks is, sadly, very common. Indeed, the whites have always banked on blacks' stupidity. Malcolm X spent a good deal of his time exposing to blacks how ridiculous and foolish blacks were. Malcolm X was a real leader because he criticised not just the whites, not just the Negro leaders, but the masses of blacks as well.

I should expand the above point a little. The Negro leaders apparently believe the masses blacks can succeed only if Democrats are Presidents. Well, since 1952, there's been 11 President elections. Seven have been won by Republicans, four by Democrats. What sense does it make for blacks to tie their fortunes on a Democratic President being in power? And when a Republican gets in power, then it's supposed to return blacks to square one? This is an awful example of misleadership that's costing black lives. In the last ten years, over 100,000 blacks have been murdered by other blacks. By comparison, the US's ten year war in Vietnam killed only 59,000 Americans!

There's a lot I can write exposing this, but, once again, space prohibits further comments. The reader must simply understand that Malcolm X's, Marcus Garvey's, and Martin Denlany's position was that blacks must financially and economically invest and work for themselves.

The results would be profoundly, profoundly, profoundly different. Just today, instead of abandoning blacks, African Americans are fully capable of investing one billion dollars a week into themselves. That's 52 BILLION dollars a year. Without asking for any new laws. Any white support. Any politics. With this funding and commitment, the many diseases infecting the black communities would mostly vanish.

Blacks would take a seat in the world of productivity. There would be too much work to do for murder and social dropout. Every black talent, skill and positive efforts would find an outlet, would be rewarded.

Blacks would work for blacks, not trying to please whites to become a token, defanged black in a white environment. Also, one of the implications of the African American nationalist success means that many of the horrors in Africa could have been by-passed because of the role African Americans would play. The reader can't begin to understand just how different it could be if blacks invested in themselves rather than in whites. The world would be so, so different for those of African descent.

This is The True Meaning of Malcolm X.

NOTES

1. Printed July 16, 1993.
2. Printed July 30, 1993.
3. Printed August 13, 1993.
4. Printed September 3, 1993.
5. Printed September 17, 1993.
6. Printed October 1, 1993.
7. Printed October 15, 1993.
8. Printed October 29, 1993.
9. Printed November 12, 1993.
10. Printed December 3, 1993.

MALCOLM X: A MORAL GIANT

Six Essays

by Don Steele

Published in the *Community Voice Newsjournal*, which is distributed in 22 states from January 1994 - August 1994

Editor's Note: These articles were originally published as an epilogue to previous essays; hence, the mention of "epilogue." However, these articles may also be read as independent essays for anyone interested in the truer and deeper meanings and comprehension of Malcolm X, including his intellectual, political, economical and indeed Spiritual meaning.

I. Introduction

The previous 10 part series, entitled "The True Meaning of Malcolm X," to which this Epilogue is being appended, represents only a certain level of comprehension, a level and way of viewing phenomena (events). That view or level can be called the political-historical analysis view. Taken by itself it is likely to be misconstrued, despite my warning in the 2nd article of the series where I stated that it was in the Divine Will, and in my subsequent article 6 where I present the Divine Mind as the true Cause and true analysis.

In a way, we can think of this political-historical analysis as a macro view or external causality. Whereas the Divine Mind represents the micro view or inner Causality. If this macro view presents itself as the root Causality, which is what a materialist philosophy like Marxism or any theory from a political science department in the universities pretends, then this is in fact a false view, a false Causality. It's just a lie.

Therefore, it's my purpose in this Epilogue to present matters from a micro level, and for this purpose it's necessary to move into deeper territories of the Divine Mind. It's necessary to take up the Spiritual Principle of the Divine Mind, and to refute the material causality of the political-historical view, which philosophically can be referred to as the political materialist philosophy. his political materialist analysis, or external view, is in opposition to the Spiritual Philosophy or inner view.

As such, given this basic opposition, it is consistent to identify this political materialist philosophy with satan's or the devil's philosophy, i.e. with falseness, deception and lies. Whether or not there actually literally exists a satan or devil need not concern us here, since our use of these terms is as symbols. The use of these literary symbols to convey certain oppositional, negative and philosophical ideas is economical and fully realized by these familiar terms.

Further to this, I must point out that this political materialist philosophy, which is satan, is the very philosophy believed in and acted on by nearly everybody. That's because satan represents and means physical existence itself!! This is the shocking meaning of satan, something not understood at all by the various preachers and others pretending to know and speak about God. With this key, one immediately can gain a deeper understanding of the Christ's conflicts with satan.

I suppose at this point I should reveal an important matter about myself, since in the previous series I explained my teenaged Marxist political beliefs and my personal involvements with Malcolm X, and how my political mentor, with whom I lived a few years along with his wife, was the editor of "The Autobiography of Malcolm X," published both the first book on Malcolm's speeches, and the first political book on Malcolm's last year. All of which despite the fact that he was a Jew and a white Marxist.

I also mentioned the fact that I self-published my first book when I was 18 on Chinese philosophy, where I utilized the historical materialist philosophy of Marx to view the unfolding of Chinese thought and sages. The following year I wrote an even larger book on the philosophy of African history before 1500 A.D. I was a Marxist philosopher.

What held my attention to Marx, unlike for most others, was the fact that Marx was first and foremost a philosopher, something not recognized by most people, even Marxists; or if so, given a short mention. What others were interested in, including my political mentor, was Marx's politics and economic reorganization of the world. But I was a philosopher even before the age of 16 when I became a Marxist. At the age of 12 I declared that I am a philosopher! I have not changed in that declaration.

But as a young 12-year-old philosopher I had a definite philosophical problem that interested me. My question was the existence of God. Did God exist, or was this just a lie? From my very brief study of world religions, I'd concluded that religions were created for moral purposes and their modus operandi was to threaten punishment for wrongdoers after death either in a hell or worst state of reincarnation, or reward those who towed the line, in either a heaven or a better state of reincarnation. What I wanted to know was whether there was anything behind this? Whether nature and laws were sufficient explanations for the existence of the universe? Whether there really is a

God or is this simply another Santa Claus story told on a much bolder and grander scale but told for the same reason: to control human behavior for the purpose of social well-being?

I astonished my elders by questioning the validity of my Baptist faith in view of the fact that I had no privileged position to know this was true vis-a-vis the alleged truths of other faiths. With my so-called beliefs I had had absolutely no input. I only believed what my family happened to have given me. I point out that if I were born in India I'd be a Hindu or Buddhist, in Saudi Arabia, a Muslim, in a Jewish family, I wouldn't believe in Jesus Christ. How do I know my beliefs are true?

No one could answer my questions satisfactorily because these questions, which appeared to me to be very obvious and necessary thoughts had never really entered their heads; or if so, nothing worth thinking much about. The lame attempt to refer to Biblical scriptures was refuted by my pointing out that these different religions themselves had different scriptures, so whose scriptures are true, if any? Thus, I began my philosophical pursuits, and my agnostic stage at the age of 12. In point of fact, it's a very rare "believer" of any faith who's capable of honestly answering these questions. I've never met a "believer" who can.

Karl Marx, however, did answer many of my questions, and so I became an atheist and absorbed deeply his version of the political materialist philosophy. However, I came to Marx through politics since at 14 I became politically aware and at 15 I entered politics as a radical black nationalist. I then a year later elevated my studies and understanding through Marxism. Although I thought very highly of Malcolm X, I was never attracted to his Islamic religion, which I took like all religions to be ignorance.

I stayed in politics for 12 years, and I worked without pay. I didn't know it then that the Divine Mind had selected me as one of Its philosophers, and that the questions I faced and asked, and the time living with my political mentor and an adherent of the political materialist philosophy were all for my understanding and proofs. It was left to me to prove who I am, and my true interest in the truth. Something confessed by so many. But nearly everyone is defeated by the political materialist philosophy, which monopolizes ideas of existence and life.

I don't mean that most people are confessed atheists. But I do mean that most Westerners, at least, believe in the political materialist philosophy, and the religion they confess faith in is simply a cover and veneer for their version of the political materialist philosophy. They're phonies and liars. Much of their "true" religion is fully analyzed and explained by Marx. Because what held me so strongly into believing Marx's system was not so much the lies of his system, but the many truths Marx revealed. The insidious problem was that like any fish I couldn't separate the worms of truth from the hook which carried these truths.

My knowledge of the Divine Mind, therefore, and as the Divine Mind's philosopher must not be miscontrued to mean I now disown the many truths Marx revealed, particularly the truths about religion. It doesn't mean I believe the fables and myths, the errors and childishness, the parochialism and sectarianism of those confessing God. Frankly, I don't believe generally in the sincerity of the preachers and priests or imams. I believe, like Marx asserted, that they're just reflections of the material and political interests, the class, clique and personal financial interests of the ones speaking, and generally they're preying on the ignorance of the people. The worst liars and the biggest hypocrites are the so-called Christians. From my personal experience I've never met or seen anybody -- NOT A ONE -- who professing Christianity didn't prove to me to be a terrible liar, which is satan.

I should also point out that as a Spiritual Philosopher I'm not to be confused with a preacher. In over three and a half decades as a philosopher, I've never made a penny from this. Preachers' livelihoods are dependent on receiving donations. They're also committed to supporting a certain set of beliefs, many of which are just cultural myths and expressions. Preachers have a limited concern-- if any--with the truth. Philosophers are in a better position to deal with truth since they uphold reason and facts, although if they're dependent in their livelihoods to be philosophers, then they too are compromised by the political materialist philosophy. Nobody, however, is completely free. But a rare few are a lot lot freer than the masses, and the mass of preachers and philosophers.

What I recognized as I started out as a young 12-year-old philosopher, that religion is a function of the moral principle, becomes a universal sea by which we can abstractly stitch together various religions and spiritual streams and rivulets. At least we can say, there's never been a religion which hasn't made morality or Freedom (requiring morality) a center of teaching, despite the great differences between religions.

Sitting within this morality sea therefore means we're sitting within the territory of the Divine Mind. And it is from the seat of this dimension we confirm that Malcolm X was a moral giant. Further, that with the assassination of Malcolm X came the negative spiritual reverberations which sentenced and doomed millions of blacks, even those far offshore of America. The bullets which gunned down Malcolm X spiritually are also the bullets presently gunning down hundreds of thousands of blacks throughout the black communities. Because directions of leadership does make a difference in people's lives, and normally, for generations to come.

This Epilogue will present and explain the Spiritual Philosophy, which, as stated above, is in conflict with the political materialist philosophy. This Philosophy is opposed by all those who believe in the latter philosophy. Particularly this true Spiritual Philosophy is strongly opposed by the black masses and their political materialist leaders. Notwithstanding, this Truth is proven to be the Truth since it's the same inner Philosophy and Words revealed by all GENUINE Spiritual prophets, saints, Holy books, scriptures, beliefs and systems: the same offered by all religions, among all tribes and races of people, in all geographical territories, however remote, and whatever their stage of human development. There is nothing parochial and conditional about this Spiritual Philosophy.

To be perfectly clear: by "GENUINE" I mean teachings with which an identifiable group of people embraced, lived, and structured their societies. Further, that a group's teachings' genuineness is confirmed by its continued existence for at least 300 years. This 300 year time distinction, while somewhat arbitrary since I could say 200 years, is nevertheless, conceptually paramount because deceitful people and false teachings often come to the fore or exist as a clique or cult within society for a time. But their moral corrosion and falseness will eventually take their toll and destroy that society or themselves, ordinarily in less than 100 years. The central purpose of all genuine moral teachings is the continuation, health and well-being of a society's variety. This is how truth or good is often interpreted. Conversely, death, destruction, sickness and ill are identified with falseness or evil.

The next article in this Epilogue will lay the deepest foundations for this Spiritual Philosophical view which will be explicated in the 3rd - 6th articles. A Philosophical view which explains why the present devastating black social statistics are not accidental but necessary; a view which condemns the present Negro leaders, who're opposed to the Eternal Truth taught by this omnipresent Spiritual Philosophy, insisting as they do on satan's political materialist analysis, while this Spiritual Philosophical view supports the claim that Malcolm X was a moral giant.

PART 2[2]

2. Philosophical Foundations

Marx divided (essentially Western) philosophy into two major and opposing camps. The first and overwhelmingly dominant camp are those who believe in God, whom Marx labelled as "idealists"; and the opposing camp, of which there have been very few takers, are the atheists, whom Marx called the "materialists."

There are problems with these terms since Marx wasn't really familiar, regrettably so, with non-Western philosophy. Be that as it may, we'll accept this distinction for purposes of continuing. It probably comes somewhat as a surprise to most readers who believe in God to realize that they are philosophically classified as "idealists." But this term idealism has not the same meaning one often hears when people say, usually referring to someone young, "s/he's an idealist."

This vulgar and commonplace distortion of philosophical idealism usually means someone is naive and believes that things are essentially good, and bright and pleasant; or, believes one's goodwill efforts will be appreciated. "Such a person hasn't awakened to the harsh realities of this world," is the common and patronizing feeling about idealism.

But the idealism labelled by Marx has nothing to do with this caricature.

The Buddha, e.g., would fall into Marx's idealist camp, but the Buddha, after his famed "Awakening," or "Enlightenment," that is, his Buddhahood, presented to the world his "Four Holy Truths" about physical life. The first of these Truths states, in effect, that earthly life itself is hell, that it is continual and unending suffering! The Buddha presented an extremely pessimistic view of material life which far surpasses even those not considering themselves, in the above vulgar sense, idealists.

So, to better understand Marx's division, I present the following philosophical physical differences in beliefs concerning "reality":

a.

This chair I'm sitting in, this table which holds my computer, this computer on which I type, this person typing, this room in which all these exist, etc. would all vanish if there were no one observing us: The "etc." continues to include all physical existence, all atoms, and sub-atomic particles, as well as the solar system, the countless stars and galaxies, the entire universe would vanish. Each particle's very physical existence is impossible without someone observing it. To repeat, the universe's very physical existence is possible if and only if there's somebody observing it and all of the universe's parts. Nothing can physically exist at all without an observer.

The preceding theory is called idealism. Conversely, materialism theorizes that this computer, etc. will continue to exist if no one observed them. Marx believed the universe can exist without ever needing an observer, and it existed long before consciousness evolved in it.

Since most readers fall into the camp of idealists, their philosophical position is that the universe vanishes without an Observer, which they hold to be God. This idea of observer (thought) = existence and no observer (no thought) = non-existence is not so pointless and out of place in modern theoretical physics as one might imagine. Elements of this debate surfaced this century in conflicts between scientific giants trying to resolve theoretical problems in quantum mechanics. Debates are still raging.

No less of a figure than Einstein was pushed aside by the majority of physicists over questions like whether or not a physical quantity like quantum spin or a localized particle exists when no one observes it. Einstein, accused of "naive realism" refused to believe human observation is necessary for physical phenomena to exist. Very recent breakthroughs in experiments, however, have supported Einstein's opponents. I myself am writing a 1200 paged mathematic Critique of Twentieth century theoretical physics with creative solutions and predictions supporting the idealist position, although this Observer isn't terrestrial consciousness.

Nevertheless, it probably still isn't clear the meaning and usage of the term "idealism." If the physical universe exists in virtue of being observed, and cannot physically exist without being observed, then the universe's physical existence is clearly something dependent rather than something independent. Further, this dependence status means the universe's "reality" is a false reality. As a minimum, the true reality must be that on which the universe is dependent. That is to say, that which is independent gives existence to or creates the dependent universe, like a dependent puppet with respect to the puppet master.

For example, if one discovered the people and scenes s/he was watching and thought were "real" turned out to be a film (or hologram), then these real scenes and people lose their "reality," since they're dependent on the film for their existence. As a minimum, reality must be in that film, but if the film is also dependent then reality, as a minimum, is transferred again to that on which the film is dependent, etc.

In the final word, it is the Observer and not the universe, which is Real. The universe is dependent on and exists through the Divine Mind as the Divine Mind's Thoughts or Ideas. Thus the reason for the term idealism.

b.

The preceding, however, doesn't prove the case for idealism. Previously, I cited historical prophecies, some predicting events and persons centuries ahead of their births as proof. But here we must provide a more elevated and strictly philosophical proof of the Divine Mind.

Most materialists like Marx and many scientists say that the universe exists in virtue of natural laws, and that the idea of an Observer as necessary for the universe to exist and function is simply a non-sequitur, a deus ex-machina. In a common word: superfluous. To be superfluous in science means to not exist. However, there is a fundamental flaw in this reasoning which philosophy has long uncovered but the sense of this Critique hasn't been understood, neither by Marx nor most academic philosophers and certainly not by your ordinary scientists, genius or not.

Because when one goes into details about this belief in natural laws as the Cause of the universe and all its actions, one again comes up with idealist results: Namely, the physical entities themselves, the actual mass and matter, the protons and neutrons of a nucleus of an atom, which themselves are composed of quarks and other particles, and the electrons which orbit this nucleus, forming the atom, from which comes the chemical elements by which the macron world is built, composing our human bodies, as well as the millions of billions of galaxies and stars formed from hot gasses, are all themselves dependents: Not one is independent of the natural laws. Yes, dependent on natural laws.

Hence, as demonstrated above about all dependencies, by these masses' dependency on natural laws, the physical universe necessarily loses its "reality," which is transferred, as a minimum, to the natural laws themselves. Natural laws or just laws become the "reality."

The proof laws are truly the "reality" is that laws possess superior properties entirely lacking in empirical matter. Most importantly, laws can make predictions whereas empirical events can't. The high point of science, in fact, is to be able to make predictions when there's been absolutely NO experience or previous knowledge of a physical event. Modern science's glory are the predictions of hitherto unsuspected physical elements, events and relationships because of discovered laws. Nobel prize winners in physics today nearly all win by either having theoretically made such predictions or experimentally confirmed other theorists' predictions. The most famous of all scientific predictions which has most dramatically changed our world in all its dimensions is Einstein's famous discovered law, E-MC2, on the basis of which was built the atomic bomb!

Further examples can be shown proving the dependency of physical matter to laws' "reality," including the fact that entities come into physical existence in virtue of laws, and during existence their movements and possibilities are determined by laws, and their existence ceases or is transformed according to laws. Hence, there's simply no consistent way given these facts natural laws support the theory physical matter represents "reality," i.e. matter exists on its own or by itself. One is forced to say that laws are the "reality," and, in fact, create physical matter, since the universe's existence is entirely dependent on laws.

So, where does this acceptance leave us? It leaves us asking the critical scientific question, since laws are the presumed "reality," and the physical universe is not: Exactly where do these natural laws exist?

We certainly can't back away from this question, but must move forward. Because it makes no sense whatsoever given the above demonstrable properties of laws to turn around and say, "Yes, but laws don't exist." Nevertheless, if this were the correct answer, "laws don't exist," then it is the correct answer moving forward, not turning back. Moving forward by uncovering laws' dependency on a prior non-physical existence as Reality, but not by turning backward by denying what we've already proven.

Where do laws exist? This capital question must be answered. As a first clue we ask how do we know anything about laws? Where and how do we perceive laws? What crashes down on our consciousness is the awareness that there is a major difference in how we get knowledge of laws versus knowledge of physical matter. With the latter, our knowledge comes through one or more of the five senses: seeing, hearing, feeling, smelling, tasting. But laws are not "sensory" and so it's impossible to gain knowledge of laws through any of our senses!

In fact, our knowledge of laws comes entirely through the mind, and stays entirely in the mind. Our answer is forced: Laws' being (ontology) or "reality" is of Mind. There's no escaping this conclusion.

c.

The universe functions according to the Divine Mind's laws, but each physical entity has its own branches of laws to which it's subjected within the overarching laws controlling all entities. Physical matter itself is not static but moves and evolves. There are whole life cycles of planets, stars and galaxies, and, presumably, universes. On our small dust there are geological laws leading to biological laws, leading to humans. And humans lead to historical laws, sociological laws, and psychological laws. Humans also lead to Spiritual and moral lawgivers.

It's an unappreciated fact that of thousands and thousands of human societies which have come into existence and adhered for generations and generations, all are governed by moral laws, the originators of which have all claimed to have received these laws either from God, some supernatural mystical experience or meditation. Some moral lawgivers prefer to make reference to natural laws with moral laws as the parallel or extention to human society, but their claims of where they received these laws doesn't originate empirically. Some, like Confucius, may regenerate the Wisdom of the ancestors, who put forth such a claim.

The question before us is can we shrink from the idea that moral laws are expressions of Moral Law which emanates from the Divine Mind, despite the many problems that must be faced in justifying this position? The prius to this question, and the one which will consume our attention is, is there such a thing as Moral Law like there is such a thing as Natural Law? Or, is Moral Law purely an invention of man for his convenience and violations, with no more necessity than, say, a red convertible Mustang?

Because an affirmative on this issue makes the meaning of Malcolm X as a moral giant possible! The following third article in this series, building on this present philosophical foundation, will present the Spiritual Philosophical Analysis and provide the context for the confirmation of Malcolm X as a moral giant.

PART 3[3]

3. The Spiritual Philosophical Analysis

We have established strong non-religious but physical philosophical reasons to support the theory that if there is no Divine Mind then the physical universe must vanish. I will not repeat the arguments of the last article, but I must proceed, given our limited space, to the point where we left off. The question before us is, is Moral Law real or contrived?

This is a very very deep question. Marx believed that moral laws merely reflected the economic and social stages of human material evolution. Savages will have quite a different set of moral laws than barbarians. Societies which permit slavery will have a different set of moral values than those opposed to slavery. Societies which are carnivorous, particularly cannibalistic societies will differ in precepts to vegetarian societies. Etc. etc. The images of the lawgiver coming down from the mountain or from heaven giving inviolable and absolute moral laws instantly evaporate once the history of human societies is reviewed and the scales of ignorance are removed from the worshipper's eyes, says Marx.

a.

Certainly Marx has very strong historical cases, but it's impossible we can follow Marx to his atheist conclusion, which I've refuted in the previous article. One of the reasons so many believe that the Buddha was an "atheist" (which isn't true despite this prevalent belief even among many Buddhists themselves) is precisely because the Buddha believed so strongly in Laws, Moral Law and otherwise.

With the Buddha there is focus simply on Laws, and the actions of humans are consumed under a very general concept of actions. The general term used is "Karman." Accordingly, the universe of atoms along with the atoms' constructs of animals and humans follow various courses of actions, the effect of which determines future courses of actions. These actions produce our experiences. Since countless trillions of actions are being performed every micro-second, by the trillions of bodily cells, and the untold number of electrons and photons, a person will have to experience an endless number of lives to realize all the mathematically exact and necessary experiences various actions determine. But in the process of living these lives, the backlog of actions keeps getting larger and larger, and one's suffering of reincarnation or rebirth continues forever.

The idea is brought into clear relief that the individual, and not the gods or God, is what produces one's experiences, both pleasant and horrifying. This means that circumstances, environment, politics are not the root Cause of one's predicament. One's own actions in previous lives, and to some extent, the present life determined one's present, and one's present decisions and actions will determine one's future, either in this life or the life to come.

The kernel of this philosophy I call the Spiritual Analysis.

I call this the Spiritual Analysis because this is the same belief, in various clothing, held by all religious and moral systems. Confucius too was scrupulous to avoid direct associations with the Chinese gods, nevertheless, he created a moral system which has as its centerpiece the Law of Retribution. Every spiritual moral system, savage or otherwise, operates on the idea that one's actions either in the immediate present or future will result in something either good or bad for the doer.

This, simply viewed, is just an observation of how the Law of life works. Life itself requires action or work, and one will get the fruit of his/her actions. Even non-life action follows the same scenario. This is what one means by Causality.

What religion does is to apply this abstract action and Causality concept to human life and society. The notion of Justice is the expression of this Law. Now, since the operation of this Law as Justice is far from obvious in the course of human affairs, the balancing of the Justice equation is sought in life after death or in a previous existence.

But given that different religions and belief systems are not equal in rigor or consistent in applying this Causality concept beyond its rudiments, and become boxed in by other beliefs, many real questions are left unanswered in most systems. The Buddha was most conscious of this Karman concept, and thus emphasized it, although this was not the Buddha's originality. Because of this awareness, the Buddha's outlook is radically different than in the generalized Judaic traditions which emphasize God.

The Buddha stood on a higher level of Spiritual comprehension than the generalized Judaic systems (i.e Judaism, Christianity and Islam), just like the Christ stood on a higher level than Judaism or the later Islam. As such, the Buddha's system was far more rigorous and uncompromising. This revolutionary believed one must rely upon himself alone. Few, however, can travel such a difficult path alone and require the assistance of a God. Thus, the Judaic traditions like most religions in the world worship God, not for pure and noble purposes, for sure, but because worshippers want things from God. They all want the same things: money, food, health, protection, sex, progenies, success, victories, long life, heaven. The Buddha was deeper than any of these wants. Therefore, he saw no reason to worship, mention or even acknowledge the existence of God. Nonetheless, what remains essential for what the Buddha's system promises, which is the cessation of rebirth, is the Buddha's Moral Law.

b.

Granted most of my readers have no real knowledge or interest in the Buddha, but I digress on the Buddha because, much older than the Christ, he is the strongest Spiritual force in Japan and the Far East, the very countries which are making the strongest economic challenge to the West. In fact, until this century, more people in the world called themselves Buddhists than any other religious system.

But indigenous rival systems of Asia like in China the Taoist systems of Lao Tzu and Chuang Tzu support in their fashion the Spiritual Philosophical Analysis (I've already included Confucius' system), in India the various Hindu systems. Moving West, old religions like the Persian Zoroaster's Avestas, the Egyptian, Assyrian and Babylonian, the African tribes, the European tribes, the Greeks and Romans, and coming to the Americas, the Incas and Aztecs, the Native Americans, and down under, the Australian aborigines, and above, the Eskimos, all in various fashions in local myths, traditions and teachings, support the Spiritual Analysis. Thus, this provides an unexpectant proof of the Divine Mind's presence in human social formations, because what is the probability that this Spiritual Analysis could be so omnipresent in human cultures when it is so objectionable and counter to what we want to hear?

Focus again is placed on the consistency of this Analysis' application as expressed by the Buddha, while other religious systems may be less understanding. The obvious existence of external forces ostensibly independent of oneself, like earthquakes, diseases, wars and other disasters, may be truthfully ascribed to external spirits and demons, which are remedied by propitiating the good God or Spirit through prayer and sacrifice. People within those systems come to care only for the practical end results and fail to see the inconsistency of independent problems and fortunes and thus lose sight of the original unity.

On the other hand, to believe that laws or principles by themselves are the ultimate Reality, fails to recognize or answer important questions about possibilities: why laws are as they are, what keeps laws informed and functioning, or as a minimum, the mental nature of laws, which I've proven, and which also accounts for laws' teleology. The fallacy of atheist based evolutionary theories lies exposed in all such theories' inability to account for teleological results, i.e. the foreseen end results. Because a specie can't evolve various complex and inter-related organs within its own body as responses to external conditions without knowledge of its many ends. So the evolution of matter and life are Consciousness driven, which is the original evolutionary theory. (The exoteric creation myths of the Bible have no place in science but convey esoteric truths.)

c.

The generalized Judaic systems also support the Spritual Philosophical Analysis. The Koran says, e.g., "We did not do you wrong. You did yourself wrong. The good a person receives, he earned. The bad a person receives, he also earned." And, "We have destroyed many people, but before doing so we have always sent a Warner (against bad morality)."

The Old Testament is poignant in explaining the military defeats and political calamities which befell the Jews after Moses to be the result of fallen Jewish morality and practices, which is usually presented as "whoring after other gods." Prophecy is predicated on this Analysis. The Christ also offered the moral solution, and even indicated that one's sicknesses and diseases are the result of sinful thoughts and actions.

Nonetheless, despite all this Biblical evidence, which black preachers profess to believe in, blacks remain convinced that the Spiritual Analysis is a lie. They seek to blame somebody other than themselves as the Cause for their pitiful social statistics. But the Spritual Analysis says that while it's true the whites have oppressed blacks, this oppression is a Consequence of the blacks' Spiritual and moral bankruptcy, and not the root Cause for their condition.

This same difference in Analyses, the difference between Consequent political oppression appearing as the Cause vs. the Spiritual root Cause, is what separated the Christ from his Jewish contemporaries in explaining Jewish oppression by the Romans. The Jews then, like the blacks today, wanted to blame outside oppressors for their predicament. Judas didn't believe Jesus, but believed if he precipitated a conflict between Jesus and the Romans, then the Christ's divine insurrection would produce the desired result. The Jews have hailed as "Moshiachs" (Messiahs) only those who've held Judas' political analysis, most notably Bar-Kokhba who in 132-5 A.D. led a revolt against Rome resulting in a great Jewish catastrophe.

Finally, Marx's discovery of the economic-socio reflections of many moral laws, while true, nevertheless, fails to see, once a certain conscious level is reached, the invariance of the Spiritual Analysis within the changing social formations; nor does he comprehend that these societies are the gratings and prisms which refract the Moral Law's Light, resulting in a spectra of different moral codes identifying these social varieties' own vibrations and wavelengths, although the inhabitants themselves may just be consciously following their own economic self-interests, while egotistically believing their societies and moral laws are absolute because of the divine origins of them.

Bees have no conscious awareness of how/why they form hives, collect nectar to make honey, nor the how/why for the laws governing the bees' economy and life cycle. Too, bees are unconscous of their pollinating importance of life forms far removed from the beehive. Nor are lower life forms better apprised of life's symbioses which laws manage, like plants breathing carbon dioxide and releasing oxygen. But they're part of life's spectra and varieties, exhibiting each its own laws as life's refraction.

The uniqueness of humans, as a physical refraction of being "made in God's image," is unlike bees' and plants' locked-in genetic codes for behavior, humans can self-create new behavior, economies and effect changes. But this possibility for freedom carries with it possibility for error and total destruction. Hence, at the human stage appears moral laws as a response to human freedom, and its possibilities. Too, within these moral laws will always be found the Spiritual Philosophical Analysis flowing like a gold stream.

PART 4[4]

4. The Spiritual and Moral Failure of Blacks--1

In the previous two articles I have taken the reader inside the territories of the Divine Mind, and we've ascended the ladder of abstract philosophy in order to provide sound foundations and proofs of the existence of a Divine Mind, Moral Law, and the Spiritual Analysis. I will not repeat the material, and unless the reader has read these articles s/he's unprepared to understand, much less refute the Spiritual Philosophical Analysis. Particularly, its application to blacks. Namely, the Spiritual and moral failure of blacks as the Cause for the devastating black social statistics, and most noticeably, the high murder of black males, which, today, is the number one cause of death of the young blacks. This Spiritual Analysis is in direct opposition to what I call the political materialist analysis, which I introduced in the first article.

For the reader paying close attention, then it follows that to the Buddha physical existence itself is satan, whom he called Mara. I stated in that first article that the Christ also believed physical existence is satan. However, Jesus didn't have the same thoroughness of consistency as the Buddha simply because the Christ, although another radical and revolutionary like the Buddha, nevertheless, was still constrained by the limitations of the Judaic comprehension vis-a-vis e.g. the Upanishads.

Also, the generalized Hindu systems (Hinduism, Buddhism, Jainism) are really devolutionary, while the generalized Judaic systems (Judaism, Christianity, Islam) are evolutionary. The difference most noticeably is that Judaism is grounded in a consciousness of historical events, and in a conception of historical evolution. Historical prophecies are given the high mark for its proof. From the comprehension of the Christians, Jesus was the fulfillment of Judaic historical prophecies, and as such, Jesus' awaited return will mark the final fulfillment and end of history.

But from the comprehension of the rival Islam, the Prophet Mohamed was the real fulfillment of the Pentateuch's prophecy. It should be clarified, however, that the meaning of the Hebrew/Arabic word "nabi," or prophet is more general in Islam than commonly understood in Judaism or Christianity where the word refers to the ability to predict a distant future. The Prophet Mohamed had no such clairvoyance, so Islam's meaning of prophet is one who reveals scriptures, or one to whom God has spoken.

Despite these and other systems' great rivalries and differences between them, they're all unified in supporting the Spiritual Analysis, which says one is the cause of one's own circumstances either positive or negative, through one's own thoughts and actions or inactions. So, having taken the reader to a certain abstract height in the previous two articles, I will begin a descent to more recognizable terrain. However, there is still one more piece of abstraction I must indulge the reader's patience with, since the use of this as a subsequent reference will prove of great economy. This abstraction has somewhat of a mathematical shade to it.

a.

Imagine a frame, a reference frame. Within this frame is a picture, possibly a moving picture. Label this frame "A." Now imagine a second frame, which has a different (moving) picture. Label this frame "B." The picture in frame B is very different than the picture in frame A.

The question before us is, is there a relationship between frames A and B? If so, then there is an equation which translates A into B. To express this equation, we say that B is a function of A, and write it thus $B = f(A)$. The expression $f(A)$ for "the function of A" is very general because it doesn't give us any idea of exactly what the relationship (function) is. That is, if we knew what f(A) meant specifically, then we could directly translate A into B. Presently, we know only that there is a relationship, which we call the "translation equation." It might be more mathematically correct to call the equation a "transformation equation," but the term "translation" is likely to be more comfortable to the reader.

For example, suppose frame A pictures English words and frame B pictures the same words in another language, say, Arabic. Then the picture of English words in A written in the Roman script will translate the quite different pictures in B of equivalent Arabic words written in Arabic script. The translation equations will be the list of English-Arabic words one will find in an English-Arabic dictionary.

Another example, which is numeric, is currency differences between countries. Suppose A represents U.S. dollars, and B represents Italian liras. The number 100 in A might become the number 159,200 in B, or $(100)A = (159,200)B$. The translation eq. is $B = f(A) = 1592 A$. That is, whatever A is multiply it by 1592 and you will get its equivalent in Italian liras or B. Each country's currency will have a different translation equation.

b.

From the concept of translation eq., we can deduce the notion of causality eq. The term f(A) implies that as we change the picture in A we will cause B to also change its picture in a prescribed and determined manner. That is, as we change English words in A, the Arabic words in B will also change. Or, as we change dollar amounts in A, the Italian lira amounts will change in B. Thus for B to be a function of A, $B = f(A)$ means it is dependent on A and frame A is the cause of frame B.

Now consider the picture in frame A of circa 1830 in the U.S. and the deep South where a plantation owner entertains his guests. He shows off his fine carriages, grand house, fine silverware, great table, imported clothes, etc. and elegant black servants, sons and daughters educated in Europe and the East, and treasures of gold, silver and paper money.

Frame B in the same place and time shows a picture in the back of black slaves living in pitch darkness, in rags, suffering a great oppression, held against their will and made to work, work, work, etc.

I don't have to ask is there a translation eq. between A and B. Observe, however, the difference in this translation eq. between A and B than in the previous examples. While an equivalence, it's not a symmetrical but an asymmetrical equivalence. Its asymmetry is on the order of a "zero sum" equivalence. Meaning one side gains at the expense of the other, so if you add the gain of one side with the loss of the other side, the sum will be zero. There's still a causality relationship between B and A such that the picture in frame A causes the picture in frame B.

Marx presented similar frames A and B between the wealth of the capitalists and the poverty of the workers. And one can think of others. This frames A,B and translation eq. concept isn't trivial because this is all the higher mathematics, Einstein and theoretical physics are all about. It is also all that Spiritual and moral genius is about. That is, these examples are an economical way of seeing the Spiritual Analysis. In this case, frame A represents one's thoughts and actions, while frame B is the consequential results, which are one's life experiences. It's also a way of seeing blacks' social life, composed collectively of many individuals.

c.

While it is easy for blacks to see the relationship between the wealth of the slave owner and the sufferings of the black slaves, what is more important is seeing the frame A of wealthy and middle class blacks and the frame B of the suffering black masses. Is there a translation eq. between A and B here? There certainly is, despite strong denials, and this is the key which exposes the Spiritual and moral failure of blacks.

Blacks love to hear the false Negro leaders give them the political materialist analysis. This line says whites are the cause for blacks' predicament. What Elijah Muhammad and Malcolm X had proven, despite their condemnation of the role of whites in blacks' oppression, was the truth of the Spiritual Analysis. A proof which the false Negro leaders, chasing after whites, want to avoid facing at all cost.

Because Elijah and more so Malcolm had proven that one can transform oneself and other blacks from crime, violence, drugs, alcoholism, prostitution, unemployment, impoverishment, homelessness, immorality, illiteracy, despondency, early death, etc.; and from being a despised and dejected creature, without ever having to change the external white oppressive, political and social conditions! This was the miracle. With absolutely no help from whites or the government. As one of Shakespeare's characters said, "The fault, dear Brutus, lies not in the stars (the white man) but within ourselves." Whites also don't want to face these facts.

Malcolm, the true heir to Elijah, unfortunately was defeated by the jealousy and lesser goals of the officials of the Nation of Islam, and by he limitations of the fallen Elijah. It's true that Malcolm was entering more dangerous waters, making it easier to be sidetracked, but Elijah was decidedly a very myopic prophet, not seeing what everybody else saw: the great changes the Negro revolution was preordained to make. Like an ostrich, Elijah buried his head in the sand, focussed solely on the wealth he was squeezing from members and prospective new recruits. But history was determined to undermine much of the phoney escapist appeal of the Nation of Islam by permitting blacks real social and political gains.

Malcolm X stood in the best position to adjust the Spiritual Analysis to these changing social political circumstances by commanding the black revolution, taking the reins from the hands of the morally reprehensible Martin King and his strategy of black financial dependency on whites and the government, on the one hand, while permitting the wholesale evasion by blacks of their financial obligations to the black communities, on the other hand. All under the cover of "integration."

The King forces encourage successful blacks to believe, except for giving them donations to help keep them in business begging whites, they're morally free of any financial obligations to the black masses, because their success is based on their own hard work and effort. But, as a matter of fact, before the black masses broke down barriers and forced blacks' demands, the results and ability of blacks to do even harder work never met with much success from whites, nor allowed blacks into the door.

In frame A we have individual blacks making tens of millions up to 100 million dollars a year, and collectively blacks generally making hundreds of billions of dollars a year, and trillions of black dollars through the decades, all of which go to build up the white and even Japanese communities, providing white and Japanese jobs. In frame B we have the joblessness, poverty, violence, despair and negative black social statistics in the black communities. B is a function of A, or $B = f(A)$.

Nonetheless, it is still true that individual blacks must take responsibility for their own actions. But it is also an overriding hard fact that people are essentially a function of their environment. One may have the free will to go against one's environment, but statistically, regardless of race, sex, clime or time, there are only a small number who ever do so. Society's interest isn't just academic: just learn the statistical distribution of a survival probability curve; just clinically determine the probable number of survivors in a violent black inner city; just generate a computer model to show us how the curve concentrates and distributes. Different environments determine different distributions of life and death probabilities. Therefore, creating the proper moral environment is the surest way of distributing the greatest concentration of morally responsible and productive blacks. Such an environment is IMPOSSIBLE without the categorical imperative of black financial morality.

Malcolm X's morality aimed precisely to save statistically large, concentrated numbers of blacks, and not just the few who're able to prove through extraordinary efforts and heroics the truth of free will.

PART 5[5]

5. The Spiritual and Moral Failure of Blacks--2

Marcus Garvey finally had to say it. This is what he said. He said blacks themselves are the cause of their own problems, not the whites. Malcolm X said, "For the first time in history blacks had a real organization (not true the first time), but some niggers had to destroy it." Martin Delany had similar remarks to make.

In the previous series on Malcolm X I spent considerable space pointing out the black nationalist solution offered by Malcolm, Garvey and Delany. But it'd be very misleading and possibly disasterous if one believed that is the end of the story, and just from nationalism blacks will prosper. Unfortunately, life isn't that simplistic. Black nationalism is no panacea but merely directs a people to respond collectively, to economically and politically provide for themselves, which provides the basis for maximum advancement, while avoiding many of the deathtraps inherent in the King approach which are with us today.

In order for black nationalism to be a positive thrust rather than a morbidity, a self-inflicted fatal wound, moral standards and enforcements are absolutely required. First, nationalism itself must be a growth or formation from a base of international humanitarianism: an internationalist base which nourishes the nationalist formation, like a community base nourishes a family formation. Nationalism without this base leads to criminal racism and immorality. Hitler was such a nationalist. Black nationalism shouldn't be used as cover for every black thug, scum and moral bastard (like "Yahweh ben Yahweh"), for ignorant, reactionary and backward traditions, for avoiding modern challenges like science, technology, and competitive mega corporations, or for evading principles of democracy, criticism and accountability for results. Healthy black nationalism is not tribalism, nor a call to escape to a mythical past.

The strongest appeal of Islam in the modern world is its internationalism, its belief in the equality of all colors and races. This certainly had a great appeal to Malcolm X. Originally, Christianity had such a belief as well, which is the reason the first Christian Church--and the only one for about 1500 years--is called "Catholic," which means universal. Most of the Church's greatest intellectual thinkers who contributed to or formulated the Catholic Church's creeds were in fact Africans: Tertullian, Clement, Origen, Athanasius, Augustine. But in time this Catholicism became perverted in Europe. Perverted racial doctrines appeared, and all these intellects were painted as white Africans. Islam never fell down in racial matters as did the white "Christians."

Thus, with this universal Islam as its base, Malcolm X's black nationalist formation was to work towards the economic, political and cultural elevation of blacks. Malcolm X also had the moral will to elevate and liberate the masses of blacks. His will stood in remarkable contrast to the will of all the present black and white leaders, as well as to the will of the masses of blacks themselves. All are working very hard to keep the blacks down, but none are working harder at this than the black leaders and professional/successful blacks. I know this from decades of personal, virtually non-stopped outrageous experiences. I know this from black history, like with the blacks' murder of Malcom X and defeat of Garvey, and a thousand billion other episodes. I know this from this Spiritual Analysis. There's no hiding place for the blacks from this ugly Truth about themsleves. This Truth is anything but "politically correct."

In the previous article I presented the idea of frames A and B, and the translation eq. $B = f(A)$, and I gave examples. The reader is referred back to that article since I won't repeat its meaning here, but will continue with further examples.

In frame A you have proud celebrity and professional blacks who spend all their time getting as much as they can for themselves, while using the history, conditions and presence of the masses of blacks as instruments for their own personal gains. In return, they place all financial and employment needs of the black masses on the shoulders of whites and the government. Their duty is completed with lectures to young blacks on getting an education, becoming acceptable to whites, and renouncing drugs, gangs and violence. They urge: Be like them. Or, like Mike. But all their efforts, like with the Negro leaders, are characterized by being nothing so much as a complete failure, while conditions worsen.

Having this "returned back to the black masses," these blacks can now get down to the serious business of using the black masses to advance their own careers. Which means they make continued references to "blacks and racism" while trying to beat out other blacks for token slots, invitations and funding whites have made available. They stay alert that other blacks on the same track don't advance further or faster than themselves, while playing a phoney, smiling, "brothers and sisters," game.

The blacks who go into law overwhelmingly go into criminal law. Black lawyers' understanding of "take a bite out of crime," is to take their bite of the exorbitant hourly rates they charge blacks caught up in the legal system. Routinely no real work is done for their clients, nor do they care about innocence, guilt or these blacks' fates. Just the money. Making the money is not everything for these black lawyers. It's the only thing. In fact, lowering the black crime rate is very bad for business.

None of these professional and business blacks has ever given any serious financial help to any black, much less blacks, in need. It's more than enough fulfilling their civic duty to refer blacks to white agencies, or bullshit fronts they themselves establish to receive donations from whites, while conveying the appearance they're really doing something financially for blacks.

This black immorality in frame A translates for frame B into the immorality of the black inner cities: the black killings and indifference to the lives of other blacks, and the negative black statistics. $B = f(A)$.

So, far from being "role models," the Spiritual Truth is that these sucessful blacks are contributing greatly to the mass murder of blacks! I've previously pointed out how these mass murders have increased with the increase and empowerment of the black middle class and celebrities, so racism can't be the cause for the murders' rise. It's well-known that the way a middle class or professional person reacts in anger and hostility, or in stopping, blocking or professionally 'killing' his rivals is quite different than the way these same impulses will be played out by the lower classes, particularly a lower class whose moral values have been eroded.

Why is it that whites refuse to tell blacks that they should form mass black corporations, by issuing shares affordable to the masses, shares costing $5 or $10, teaching them the significance of this, and raising $1 billion a week, or $52 billion a year? This financing would solve most black social problems. Whites have created millions of such corporations. Real corporations whose real financial purpose is to raise capital by taking a little from a lot of people. Not corporations formed solely to avoid liabilities, which is the case with nearly all black corporations. This is what Garvey was doing, but no black leader has come forth with such a program since then. Malcolm X was poised to do so.

Why is it when the Republicans talk about black capitalism they're referring to just individuals getting into business with just one or a few owners? Why don't they present the same model to blacks as used by the whites the Republicans truly represent, the mass white corporations?

Because the whites don't want the blacks free. Period.

Well, then, why is it that the black elites, the businessmen, lawyers, professionals, academics who all know about corporate America and corporate Japan, why is it they don't offer this solution to the black masses? Surely, their reasons must be different than the whites?

Because these blacks don't want the blacks free. Period.

Probably not very many readers can believe this. Perhaps its shocking. But it's absolutely true. Malcolm X used to talk about how the Negro leaders were "against the black revolution. Against the black revolution!" These blacks, like the whites, simply don't want the black masses free. Granted, we understand whites' reasons. But why and how could blacks also not want the blacks free? How is this possible?

This is where the Spiritual Analysis again shows its strength and Truth. This same question can be asked in the form, how is it possible that the blacks could gun down such a great black leader as Malcolm X? This is the same question because Malcolm X represented black freedom. What other examples of this have blacks done?

I've pointed out that a black shot at Marcus Garvey, who represented black freedom during his day. But Garvey was done in by going to prison, not killed, and the ones to join with whites in putting Garvey in prison were blacks and the official Negro leaders, even long-time black freedom fighter, W.E.B. DuBois joined in this conspiracy.

During time of slavery, there were hundreds of slave rebellions, but nearly every slave revolt, including Nat Turner's and Denmark Vessey's, was betrayed by some blacks. Originally, Africans were sold into slavery by other Africans. And throughout American history, not only those struggles which have made the pages of history, but in every kitchen and rural area, in every town and city, in every church and organization, blacks secretly and openly joined with whites or just by themselves have dropped their turds to make sure that the blacks don't become free!

This doesn't mean, however, that blacks shouldn't be opposed to black moral criminals, or maintain any black whom whites are against, ipso facto, other blacks must be for. Again, life isn't that simplistic. The times, circumstances and actions present the truth.

What keeps blacks from not wanting other blacks free is usually jealousy, and/or some financial comfort these blacks are experiencing in the status quo. Black leaders need the sore conditions of the black masses to stay as leaders, so progress, if any, must be slow. Any real or rapid black solution pushes these leaders aside, or at a minimum greatly reduces their influence. Therefore, to keep their positions and cash flow, these black leaders must keep the black masses down. They always stay in fear anyway of any newcomer or upstart who has a greater appeal than themselves. Malcolm and Garvey were such victims of this black jealousy.

Even Roy Wilkins, the former Executive Director of the NAACP, was exposed as giving negative reports about Martin King to J. Edgar Hoover's FBI, which he knew hated King, an upstart who had eclipsed Wilkins as chief Negro leader. Wilkins played a phoney two-faced game with King, and secretly wanted his downfall. And I'm sure his example can be multiplied.

The professional, business, academic and other successful blacks take pride in measuring their distance from and accomplishments over the masses of blacks, and become infected with a perverse ego, convincing themselves they're really just geniuses and "all that all that." Malcolm X ridiculed this same attitude of similar blacks, "who brag 'I'm the only one (Negro) on my job. The only one in my neighborhood. The only one...'"

The best way for these egos to be nourished is if the masses of blacks stay down, so theirs can stay up and shine. Like with whites' racist cover, these blacks always stay in fear of more attractive blacks upstaging them, so they learn to play a two-faced game, claiming they have no financial responsibilities to other blacks. Compounding and exacerbating these tensions is the old serpent, the sexual component, venomously hissing, pervading and biting these egos, fears and jealousies.

Finally, the ordinary black in his inter-personal relationships and limited terrain has similar jealousy reasons for keeping down blacks like himself. He doesn't want anyone to get ahead of himself. These feelings, however, are expressed more violently and less two-faced.

6. Chickens Coming Home to Roost

Spiritual Philosophy, like philosophy generally, uses the instrument of reason. It's reason mediating on either side of itself two different spheres of experience. On this side of reason is the ordinary experience of life and the universe, the material world, which non-spiritual philosophers, the foremost of whom is Karl Marx, take to be "reality."

The other side of reason is a different Experience which isn't at all easily accessible to people; an Experience, in fact, a very very rare few ever realize, and because of which, its very existence is denied by the materialist philosophers like Marx, but which is, nevertheless, what we Spiritual Philosophers identify as Reality.

This Reality is not the same as having one's prayers answered, miraculous healings and savings, having supernormal powers and prophecies, in touch with spirits or demons, etc., although such experiences generally prove there's more to "reality" than Marx wants to admit; but few who have these experiences ever Experience Reality. However, those who do touch Reality usually have access to these lesser miracles and wonders. This Reality is prior to any physical manifestations, whatever its grade or degree, and is the ultimate source for physical existence, since, as we've seen, the definition of this Reality is its own independence and self- subsistence.

Those who touch different levels of this Reality have different names for it. The Buddha called it Nirvana; the Christ, the Kingdom of God. Great Philosopshers who touch it develop systems like Plato's World of Ideas, the Hindu Shankara's Advaita Vedanta, the Buddhist Nagarjuna's Madhyamika and Bodhidharma's Zen, Chuang Tzu's Taoism, Plotinus' NeoPlatonism, the Muslim Alfarabi's Sufism, or the Christian Aquinas's Experience stopped his philosophizing, calling his previous writings, "a pile of straw." They all affirm the Superiority of this Reality over Marx's reality. There's a distaste and disdain, in various degrees, to Marx's material reality. Christ couched this rejection in sayings such as satan is the ruler of this world, and "This is not my world."

Yet, according to Plato and Aristotle, the first and greatest of these Spiritual Philosophers, these "mystics," whose names are not familiar to us today, were the Africans, i.e. the ancient Egyptians. According to the theory advanced by George James in his "Stolen Legacy," the rest of the world received its philosophical Wisdom from this original black source. But however or to whatever extent this is true, it is still the actual Experience itself which is authenticating. Not the theories.

This Experience and not just reason or "philosophy" sees the material world as transient, changing and murderous. Negative reactions to and rejections of this material world are expressed by these "mystics" in proportion to the different levels of Reality touched by them, and in accordance to their cultures' traditions. But despite the many differences between them, they still believe in a connection, a mediation between this Reality and Marx's material reality. One cosmic branch of this mediation is called Moral Law.

What I've revealed is an identity of beliefs in all religions, in all ages, races, creeds and climes, in what I call the Spiritual Philosophical Analysis. To wit: One's conditions, both positive and negative, are the result of one's own thoughts and actions. God created good and evil only in the sense that God created the universe, but the actors precipitate the results. Different systems have different grades of consistency in this Analysis.

This Spiritual Analysis is in direct conflict with what I call the political materialist analysis, which I identified with satan's deceptive analysis. From the standpoint of the latter, the Spirtual Analysis is the original "blaming the victim" philosophy. The political materialist analysis places all the blame with somebody or something else. If one thinks about politics and politicians, s/he realizes two inseparable things: First, it's impossible to think of politics and politicians without thinking "lies and liars." Second, politics and politicians stay in conflict with others, while blaming the others for its side's problems.

Jesus' original encounter with satan is a dialogue and conflict between the Christ's conception of Reality vs. satan's reality, and the consequent Spiritual Analysis vs. the political materialist analysis. It's not a little thing that satan has control of all the political kingdoms of the world, which he offers to Christ if he rejects the Spiritual Reality.

Applying and using these ancient and contemporary teachings as a sieve to sift the Negro leaders, we now can better understand and even expect the devastating black social statistics. Virtually all the black leaders, religious and otherwise, support satan's political materialist analysis. They believe in satan's 'political correctness,' including such moral betrayal and poison as homosexuality, which is condemned by every prophet, saint and genuine Spiritual system. The roots of these misleaders' disease are self-promotion, love of easy money, while willfully financially abandoning blacks to their historic white enemies.

While there's generated talk now about morality and the loss of religion, family values, God, etc., the plain truth is there is evasion and avoidance by these same black speakers on what blacks' economic and financial obligations are to themselves. I can GUARANTEE YOU none of these other problems will ever be seriously solved without this issue confronted and dealt with. Some nationalist elements believe the problem is "integration," itself, but why shouldn't blacks live wherever they please, particularly if many black places are unsuitable? Malcolm X even while chief spokesman for Elijah Muhammad and espousing separatism didn't live in Harlem, but a white section in New York.

The real cancer is the lack of black investments in the black communities, the lack of black banks and financial institutions providing capital for black entrepreneurs, businesses and loans for consumers. The lack of a thousand mass black corporations producing a hundred thousand products, including automobiles, and services for the local, national and world markets. The lack of a black television network and serious national media. The lack of ships and airplanes engaged in international trade and commerce. The lack of tall black office buildings, hotels and architecture in every city. The lack of transforming the black communities into busy bee hives where every talent can be encouraged and nourished. All by black dollars, except for funds which augment but not replace black capital.

And the biggest LIE satan perpetrates is that blacks don't have the capital. That blacks must always look towards whites to provide, towards white corporate America, the government and white philanthropy. Meanwhile this LIE frees blacks making tens of millions of dollars a year from any black financial obligations: If anything whatsoever financial for blacks is done, it's done in the name of charity and donations. Pitiful, pitiful.

This moral shame is seen at its worst with the Reagan tax cut issue. The Negro leaders spent 12 years screaming about Reagan's tax cut on the rich. O.K. let's look at it. From 70%, rates were cut to, say, 30%. These "leaders" demanded a return to the former 70% rate. But why is it that the same leaders didn't demand with that 40% difference in taxes the mega-rich blacks invest in the black communities, which was Reagan's tax cut idea? Not donations, but investments. The VERY, VERY, VERY WORST that could result is that the rich blacks returned to the same financial situation if Reagan had never been elected. OR, if the black leaders got their demands.

This means blacks like Don King, Cosby, Oprah, etc. whose taxable income is, say, $80 M each, would before Reagan owe $56 M in taxes. After Reagan's tax cut, this amount is reduced to $24 M, or a savings of $32 M. What black has invested in one year $32 M in the black community? Just these three blacks have a total FREE $100 M per year to invest. In fact, in the last ten years blacks collectively have received an extra hundreds of billions of dollars which could have been directed towards black upliftment. The celebrities and Negro misleaders hope no one notices! Certainly, the blacks' so-called white friends are saying absolutely NOTHING about this black self-financing. And what we're talking about are black lives, lives killed and destroyed for lack of investments.

One of the many unspoken negative consequences of the disasterous Martin King--I don't have to pay--immorality embraced by the Negro leaders is that it kills and perverts black talents in all but a few limited areas. That's because black genius and talent must be filtered through a white prism of acceptability. Every black celebrity or success who's seen and congratulated in the national media must meet white approval. Approval by an oppressor with a very long and continued history of castrating/sexual fear of the black male, while sexually exploiting the black female, stifling/stealing higher black intellect and achievements, while promoting black mediocrity/degradation/docility/political acquiescence. Plus, tokenism.

This black cultural and political mass murder, the counterparts to the mass street murders, remains hidden and unrecorded, because with the Negro leaders' support the whites are able to play a phoney game of selecting and displaying the blacks they like. With smiling, white teeth showing black faces on their payrolls, the whites "cover" their dagger in a black cloth. Even genuine black talent, for employment, sells his/her talent along lines acceptable to the whites' perversions and black oppression. And for every black allowed to make money in a white corporation/production, the Negro leadership grinds out its delight about the "progress" being made.

THERE'S NO SUCH THING as a Black Republican or Democrat or a black employed by whites or the government WHO HASN'T SOLD OUT THE TRUE INTEREST OF THE BLACKS! Blacks working for whites in fact are working for whites' interests and against blacks' interest. The end result is a choking of black talent, and dead bodies in the streets. For example, notice how whites destroyed Professor Jeffries because of some truths he stated against the Jews, America's Sacred Cows. Also notice how Jeffries never made the round of the talk shows, not even the shows hosted by blacks.

It's only when the blacks overthrow the present Negro leaders, elected and otherwise, Democrats and Republicans; when blacks make the black celebrities/successes pay up and be responsible to them and not whites; when black leaders become accountable for results, when real economic and social results, and not publicity seeking, become the true meaning of leadership, can blacks ever expect recovery from their present moral sickness. This was the moral height, standard and cure of Malcolm X.

Only the overthrow of all the present Negro leaders can please and satisfy Me. Or, don't overthrow these leaders, who're Spiritual and moral germs. Keep them. But keep too the diseases of the black communities, which grow from these germs. Indeed, expect matters to grow worse. Let the reader believe what s/he wants. But the moral foolishness of the King followers who're looking for somebody, the Koreans, or anybody, anybody except blacks, to pay for blacks is like the foolish man that Christ said built his house upon the sand. Oh-h-h, how I still mourn Malcolm X.

I condemn all the Negro leaders and celebrities/successes who support this shame. Only their overthrow can Please and Satisfy Me-e-e!! And if it's asked, just who the #û%?! hell am I who must be Pleased and Satisfied? I'm simply a philosopher. One who, having practiced philosophy for 35 years, hasn't been paid. Unbought and unbowed.

I'm the one saying, "the chickens have come home to roost." I'm also the one asking the Negro leaders and America the same question that the Christ asked the Jewish leaders. And this question is Very Great because of the answer history soon gave to it after Jesus' death, an answer with which history has continued to plague the Jews all the way up to today:

"Just how do you expect to escape the damnation of hell?"

NOTES

1. Printed January 14, 1994.
2. Printed January 28, 1994.
3. Printed February 11, 1994.
4. Printed February 25, 1994.
5. Printed March 11, 1994.
6. Printed March 25, 1994.

THE ECONOMIC PHILOSOPHY OF
MALCOLM X

by Don Steele

Originally published as "Prolegomena to the
Economic Philosophy of Malcolm X" in *The
Revenge of Malcolm X and The Fruits of the Negro
Leaders*, Volumes I and II, 1998, printed in the
Community Voice Newsjournal, which is distributed
in 22 states, from July 1993 - December 1994.

PART 1[1]

"Show me thy faith without thy works, and I'll show them my faith by my works." James

This Prolegomena, or Preface as it were, prepares the reader for the 10 part series of articles entitled, "The Economic Philosophy of Malcolm X." That is, if the Divine Mind OKs giving you this, since I can't do anything without the Divine Mind's approval. Thus far, that approval has not come, and might not come. The issue doesn't at all contend on my ability to write the articles, and then to have Publisher Cordray publish them. But I've previously written, I don't have the interest to just write articles. After all, I'm not in politics nor a religious leader. I don't: associate with others. Talk to others. Laugh with others. Attend meetings. Congregate or worship with blacks. No social life. Work life. Get-togethers. People don't know me.

My only part of the Lexington economy is to pay out. Just keep paying out. I'm not paid by Lexington or Kentucky. I owe Lexington NOTHING. I owe Blacks NOTHING. I owe whites-Jews NOTHING. I owe America NOTHING. I just pay out.

This isolation or internal exile is for very good reasons. I simply DO NOT SUPPORT this God-awful economic, social, political, spiritual and moral breakdown of blacks. A breakdown which is a disease, but few know it. A disease which is supported by the Negro Misleaders. Nor do I support the whites-Jews' God-awful relationships they maintain with blacks.

Most readers easily accept as good sense my not associating and thereby supporting drug dealers and addicts. Or gangsters and other criminals. Nor would they find fault in my not being pals with perverts, hanging out with homeless or rowdy and filthy and unclean people, etc.

Well, guess what? The plain truth is I find so-called respectable people as also falling into a class of undesirables. America has consistently, continually and unabatedly cheated, robbed and dishonored the hell out of me. Denied me. And the phoney, jealous blacks have been right there supporting this against me, hoping to add me to their very long list of casualties. All of which I find to be very undesirable.

But as I near half a century of living-- although many think I'm perhaps as much as 15-20 years younger--I know the Divine Mind has its own schedule. And, ultimately, I know the only problem I've ever had, according to the Spiritual Analysis, is due to myself: if it's just desiring life.

So my interest in writing these Malcolm X articles has not been to accrue any personal, social benefits to myself. But to give understanding to effect change. And indeed since my articles began appearing last year, noticeable changes nationally have deepened. Further, as a happy coincidence, with the latest elections, the proof of the weakening of the Negro Misleaders' political hold is demonstrable.

You see, I can't live the way you do. I can't and don't work for whites-Jews. You don't care. I can't be a criminal, rob the poor, or sell drugs. A significant number of you don't care. I can't be a phoney preacher, just getting the blacks' donations. My God, I could never be something so miserable as a Negro Misleader.

On the other end: I'm much more than a barber or small shopkeeper. I can't even be an attorney. I rejected that when I qualified for law school at 19. Nor am I a teacher, although, again at 19, I was teaching mathematics in high school. I've never really been moved by money over principle and honor. Nor could many other things convince me of their truth. And many things I was convinced was truth only proved to be lies.

There's so much which society supports, too much, which my own spiritual and moral level prevents me from doing, although I'm very very far from being a St. Francis. Instead, there is just alienation. There's no place for me. Still, there are a few things I know which I believe can help you, and that, principally, is the reason I write. It's enough for me, unknown and unthanked, looking from behind the shadows, to see you learn more truth, and act on it. What you gain thereby is more freedom.

2.

The form of my alienation is certainly different than the alienation experienced by the masses of black males, particularly the young, who don't even conceptualize their problem as one of alienation. Nevertheless, I believe the root cause for both of our alienation is the same. In that sense, we are "brothers." For these others, unfortunately, too many end up dead, in prison, or live wasted, desperate and disrespected lives. I believe very strongly that if Malcolm X had lived, then there'd have been an honorable place for me and them in American society, in black society. Or, prior, if Garvey had succeeded. Or, earlier still, Delany.

But there is no place for me. That is, no acceptable place. Rodney King asked the famous question during the L. A. riots, "Can we all get along?" Yes, Rodney. But the real question is, "On whose terms?"

There's never been a problem for blacks to "get along." Simple. To get along. Go along. But go along with being what? A nigger? Someone whom whites have successfully "Lorraine Bobbicked?" Oh, no. I've had too much experience these near half century for anyone to deny it.

What is of fundamental ignorance of the King-styled Negro Misleaders is the fact that WORKING FOR WHITES simply KILLS the black males' Spirit. It's killing blacks: From this fundamental economic core of black dependency, and spiritual castration, black weaknesses flow, manifested in every area, beginning with intelligence.

Ossie Davis in his memorable eulogy at Malcolm X's funeral said that Malcolm X represented blacks' "Manhood." That has been the all-important psychology for black males in America. The stabbing pain. The unconscious neurotic (even psychotic) complex seeking conscious healing, to use psychoanalytical terms. That Malcolm X was our own "Black Shining Prince." That Malcolm X represented "Black Manhood."

But this "Manhood" is certainly not to be defined by how large one's phallus is, nor how many women one has or babies one has sired, nor how violent and murderous one can be. Nor, surprisingly, even by how much money one has. These conscious solutions to the unconscious pains are misguided and bogus and frequently fatal.

Nor is this "Manhood" simply "telling it to whites-Jews," as so many demagogic blacks want to make it. True, Malcom X lambasted the whites, but he also heaped much scorn on blacks; especially, the moral character failure of many African Americans. Still, this wasn't the whole meal, both meat and potatoes. Malcolm's negativism was just part of the plate. In retrospect, just the appetizer. Because the meal itself involved real, practical and concrete spiritual and moral transformation. The meal/work itself was something wholly and completely POSITIVE.

The core of Malcolm's "Manhood" was a demand to be ECONOMICALLY FREE OF WHITES. This essential point has been plowed over like unwanted weeds by nearly everyone. Malcolm X's economics is just the OPPOSITE of everything the Negro Misleaders have been advancing. It's against their entire politico-socio-economic raison d'etre. And we know as a certainty what Malcolm X's economic philosophy was because he stated it so. He stated it while a member of the Nation of Islam, and he stated it again after his split from Elijah, and again after his return from Mecca; and on the very day of his assassination, he was going to state it once more, with details.

It's past time blacks started looking at slavery for its true meaning and import. That is, slavery was an economic system whereby blacks worked for whites. Freedom from slavery doesn't mean only freedom of movement, and freedom from being whites' chattel. True freedom means not working for whites at all. All truly positive social and political dimensions flow from such black freedom. Including the black males' "Manhood."

But the reverse is not true. Thus the female Jew baseball owner could still state that her black players were just "million dollar niggers." LIke owning million dollar horses. That's the capital difference. That's the difference in meaning of Delany, Garvey, and Malcolm X vs. Martin King and the gang of paid for Negro Misleaders.

Pseudo black nationalists who may wear African-styled clothing, make a lot of noise denouncing capitalism and imperialism, but whose economic solution is: whites must give blacks "reparations." government programs, "affirmative action" are as much of the problem as the Negro Misleaders.

Added to these are the "nationalists" who pervert this non-dependency on whites-Jews into non-dependency on white-Jew Democrats, but working for whites-Jew Republicans is all right. There's nothing at all in common substantially with Malcolm X and a Clarence Thomas and black Republicans. That's because Malcolm's last statement on the issue was, "Before there's any black-white unity, there must first be black unity." In simple words, Malcolm X didn't seek after white politicans to fund and promote him, or give him access to white country clubs. Malcolm X wasn't an opportunist or cheap careerist!

3.

Before the controversy of blacks' inferiority was recently re-ignited and given much publicity in the media, in one of the Malcolm articles I exposed the fact that the Negro Misleaders' programs represent a capitulation to the belief in blacks' inferiority. How apropos:

In a letter to "Community Voice" I gave the appropriate response blacks should assume. (It seems that this theory has suddenly disappeared from the media after the appearance of my letter. A happy coincidence.)

However, there are blacks who believe the dog's theory can be rebutted by emotional appeals to the pyramids of ancient Egypt, and to mindless rattle that whites have never built anything greater than these tombstones, nor has civilization advanced much beyond ancient Egypt, etc.

Martin Delany, the father of modern black nationalism, was amongst the first to emphasize African history and achievements. This was still during the time of slavery. Garvey emphasized it, and Malcolm X stated that the secret of the Black Muslims' success was this emphasis on Africa. Thus, the black nationalist forces have throughout been the greatest promulgators of African's achievement legacy.

Nonetheless, such references hardly refute the dog's theory. There are many reasons for this, but the bottom line is: Where is your pyramid? Before I left Paris, France, where I lived, there was great publicity given to a new art construction for which the Chinese architect, I. Pei was commissioned. In Paris, which proclaims itself "the most beautiful city in the world," and where art is taken very, very seriously, a major construction such as I. Pei's work is of great significance. Pei built a pyramid, which now is one of the great art attractions in Paris.

Where is your pyramid? That, in essence, is what the dog's theory is asking. Logically speaking, the achievements of the ancient Egyptians can never translate into African American achievements. I don't include here the many other historical and lineage problems, which, in truth, are also fatal to such efforts: For even if we agreed that the Egyptians were black, it doesn't follow that the completely modern ideas of "race" translate back to the racial beliefs and practices then.

I wrote about what the American "melting pot" idea did. Previously, identifying people on the virtue of skincolor alone never existed. Even Hitler believed in different white races, and so his "Aryan" concept didn't mean whites in the American sense. Hitler attacked Russia because he believed the "Slavs" were an inferior race to the "Aryans." A concept very difficult for Americans to understand.

Africans never believed that the same skin color made one the same people. Neither did the ancient Egyptians. That means a white Egyptian's "race" would be Egyptian, whereas a black born outside of Egypt would not. African Americans trace their real ancestry not to the died out "race" of black Egyptians but other races. Again, to lump people by skin color is a very recent idea, which can't even be genetically supported.

But, as stated, I don't mean these historical and lineage fatalities, which, being too difficult to understand for most Americans, I can simply ignore. I mean such pyramid references are plainly illogical and can't refute the dog's theory, even if we generously accepted everything the blacks want to hear connecting themselves with the ancient Egyptians.

That's because there are many children who are born retarded and crippled, although neither parent is. It's illogical to argue that a child isn't retarded and crippled, or deaf, dumb and blind, because its parents aren't. It's even more illogical to point out its grandparents weren't either. But to go back a 1,000, 3,000, 5,000 years to argue about the present child is patently absurd. There's a song which sings, "Moma may have, and papa may have,

but God bless the child who's got his own."
Where's your pyramid?

We've all seen miniature horses which are about the size of dogs. They were bred down from not-so-distant ancestors who were regular sized horses. Are African Americans a bred down race, mental and moral runts, although physically and sexually powerful, the results of experimental slave breeding, even if we accepted this ancient Egyptian lineage? Where's your pyramid?

The meaning of Delany, Garvey and Malcolm X's emphasis on African achievements was not to just furnish retorts to whites, thereby freeing blacks to continue in their dependency, laziness and dullness: livening up only for church hollerings, songs and dances, ball games, violence, laughter and sex. Or political rallies. It was meant to motivate blacks to build their own pyramids. Building pyramids today symbolizes building corporations and companies, architectual wonders and cities, technologies and innovations. It symbolizes blacks investing in themselves, gaining economic freedom and regaining for black males their true "Manhood."

PART 2[2]

"If ye suffer, ye suffer because of yourself."
The Buddha

Malcolm X claimed that the Negro Misleaders of his day were like novocain, a medicine dentists used to deaden the pain of their drilling. Their real purpose was simply to pacify the black masses. These Misleaders had no interest at all in stopping the drilling, i.e., the painful suffering, but their job was to teach blacks how to suffer "peacefully."

These Misleaders included what Malcolm called, "religious Uncle Toms." He said these Misleaders never "incited you, or excited you." That is, these Misleaders never inspired blacks, especially the young. They were like conductors who sold tickets to cramped, overcrowded, hot and stuffy, sleeping quarters on a slow moving train to nowhere. Your only prospect in life was the hope that the pieces of human meat lying next to you in your boxcar might provide you with some pleasure along the way.

As novocained pacifiers, these Negro Misleaders worked both sides of the street. They also pacified their white-Jew bosses, assuring them that all was well amongst the blacks. Or, could be made better if they had a "little more to work with." "For a Few Dollars More."

An outstanding difference (among about 50) between Malcolm X and Martin King was that Malcolm knew the anger of the black communities and predicted the black riots which became fashionable after his death in the 60's. King denied it, and rushed to pacify whites. Ironically, after King's assassination over 100 cities went up in flames, and this fear, not the peaceful demonstrations, is what moved white America, coupled with the worldwide anti-colonial revolutions with full Communist support.

The Negro Misleaders, palpably proven to be liars, changed costumes as quickly as Superman, and became firemen. Their job was to douse the black fires, then enrich themselves at every favored opportunity, while insinuating themselves into ever higher layers of white-Jew power. They used the black masses to feather their own and their cronies' nests.

2.

So what constitutes black leadership? Pacifiers and firemen? Endless fake meetings, marches and rallies with appeals for calm, God and government aid? I ask these questions because the recent disturbances in Lexington following the police shooting death of a young black focussed attention on what's classified as black "leadership" (sic) in Lexington.

One doesn't have to be a genius much less a prophet to predict the continued spread in Lexington of the social diseases that are affecting other black communities across the country. So, about five years ago, after living a couple of years in Lexington, although I have no social involvement, I volunteered to one, "You know Lexington is not a bad place, but unfortunately as the years unfold, you're going to find the slow deterioration of Lexington's young blacks and an increase in drugs, violence and lawlessness, much as in many other parts of the country."

One doesn't have to be a genius or prophet to know this. One only has to stop living in dreams that the local so-called "leaders" offer anything to the young blacks except novocain and pacification. Which include government programs and jobs extorted from the white business community.

Of course, I'm not a stranger to real riots, ither. As a matter of fact, the big Detroit riots of 1967 started about 3 blocks from where I lived. It was the Mother of all black riots until the recent Rodney King riots. I was in it. "Burn, baby burn," was the cry. It was all burning buildings. Flames and looters. The government poured in tanks with mounted machine guns, and white soldiers marched through with bayonets on their lethal weapons. Firing at snipers, or anybody who made a bad move. I was in the riots of New York City after King's assassination a year later. I was also in the riots in Buffalo.

During all these hot times, I always thought about Malcolm X. I'd think about the last of four times I met him in Detroit, exactly one week before his assassination. I thought about the few moments I shared with him alone in his hotel room after his speech. His embarrassment that only I, a teenager, who offered to defend him with my life, came forth in face of imminent danger (his home had been fire bombed that day) from about 50 threatening Black Muslims at his speech. He declined the request I stay with him and act as a guard while he slept that night.

I still remember what was on TV in that hotel room. I stayed there while he went out to eat with Att. Milton Henry, his sponsor for the evening. It was a John Wayne movie. I immediately saw the contrast. Between this fake hero, the actor John Wayne, and the real hero who was Malcolm X. My real leader, who was Malcolm X. I have subsequently come to realize that these last moments with Malcolm X was a gift that the Divine Mind had given me. At that time, as I've written, I was a Marxist atheist.

So, do these local "leaders" inspire anybody, except weak clones like themselves? I mean, do they inspire black Manhood as I defined it in Part 1 of this Prolegomena? Or, is theirs only a program of delivering blacks into the hands of whites-Jews, who finish the "Lorrain Bobbick" job.

Of the trillions and trillions of brain cells in these "leaders'" heads, is there one, just one cell which has a meaningful program of emancipating blacks from economic dependency on whites? This is sinful.

Why? Because blacks don't want to invest any of their own money into other blacks. You love blaming everybody but yourselves for the consequences of this sin. You lie you don't have any money. That's because you prefer spending it on luxury cars, consumer items and fun living, or just giving it to the whites-Jews for safekeeping. Let the whites-Jews/Asians be real, responsible adults building things and employing millions with blacks' savings. You'll settle for interest and dividend payments. You only pretend to be adults. In truth, you're man-child and woman-child, and this is of your own accord. Your misleaders reflect who you are, and what you are.

3.

I have very little space here, and can only be very brief. Just indicative of what real vs. placebo leadership is about a la the Economic Philosophy of Malcolm X applied to Lexington.

There are about 32,000 (or 32 K) blacks in Lexington.   Real leadership would establish a capital fund goal of $20 million (or $20 M) per year. That works out to about $12/head per week. Naturally, this 32 K includes kids and the elderly. But most blacks are capable of investing $20/week or more. Leadership would direct blacks' attention to the dollars spent on alcohol, tobacco, gambling, entertainment, high priced cars, etc.

This is an investment.   Not a donation. Accounts are given. Corproations are established. I know (from my work as an "international financier"--a pretentious title) in the international banking market, without any risk to capital, how 100% APR can be had for that $20 M. After paying commissions, taxes, and 10% dividends to investors, that leaves 50%, or $10 M to work with. Understand, the $20 M is safe and undisturbed. And that 10% return to investors is more than bank CDs' 4%.

During this process, blacks are put to work reviewing and analysing various businesses. Which are the businesses which are feasible for blacks to start, based upon a dozen or so factors? This work includes getting all information and contacts on expertise, supplies, training, etc.

A good example would be auto repair shops. Blacks own cars and need servicing. The decision is reached to open 10 black auto repair shops, under a trade name, like "Black Town Auto Repair." Perhaps it requires $250 K per shop. That's $2.5 M of your $10 M. That's one, but there are at least a 100 businesses here in Lexington that blacks can get into.

Establishing financial institutions would be a priority. Black banks, insurance companies, venture capital groups. Favorable loans for college and job training would be guaranteed. Blacks who have good ideas for businesses will be encouraged and get black funding. But blacks should not, as the Bible says, "put a stone before a blind man." Blacks must adapt things to their own peculiarities and needs, and design things to genuinely help other blacks, without being made fools of. These are not government programs, but private black capital.

Example: Black management companies should be established. A would-be owner of a new business needing funding would effectively work first for the management company. This company would be assigned to work with this black, knowing who s/he is, and what his/her level of skills are. Because a black has a criminal past can't be a taboo for this black development. On the contrary, this effort will make special appeals to such elements. This is the opposite of whites-Jews, who want only safe black geldings and placebo leaders.

The management company will insure that monies are not either stolen or foolishly wasted. This is because the owner doesn't have control of the funds. An account is established for him/her, and all payments are reviewed and made by the management company. The owner receives salary payments for his/her services. On-sight inspections and continual input are given by the management company.

A contract will have been signed giving the details, terms and understanding to the owner. It may take up to 5 years of such management/training before the new company is completely in the hands of that black. Owning the company requires buying it. During the chosen business apprenticeship period, if that person doesn't work out, then instead of the whole affair being a waste of money, some other black can be put in place who wants to own the business.

A black advertising council would be formed. Their business would be to see that blacks, and the general public, are specifically aware of these businesses. They would advertise in the media. Weekly newsletters and sales advertisements would be distributed to black churches, social outlets, the Community Voice, and by direct mail.

Now, each year, you're adding another $20 M to your capital base, and another $10 M of its interest invested in Lexington. So, after two years you've got $40 M in untouched, capital and $20 M interest invested plus the first years' $10 M for a total of $30 M invested in Lexington. After one

Presidential term of 4 years, you've got a safe, untouched $80 M capital base, and $100 M ($40 + 30 + 20 + 10) invested in black businesses, loans and employment, which will be returning high investment profits.

After 12 years, the time period blacks did nothing but complain about Reagan-Bush's government cutbacks, blacks can have in Lexington $240 M in untouched capital, plus $780 M invested in blacks. All this for just $12/week per black. Of course, the total capital investments will be many times this, since blacks will invest more money seeing the great multi-dimensional results, plus re-invested profits and interests. As a stoned hard cash Reality, blacks in Lexington after 12 years could have over $5 billion in total capital investments.

Land area in Lexington can be bought which will concentrate an array of black businesses, supermarkets, restaurants, cinemas, theaters. Just like many cities have Chinatowns, this mall can be known as Blacktown. Naturally, black businesses will be located around the city, but Blacktown will be an inspiring center/magnet for black shopping and entertainment.

Instead of you complaining about not having a radio station, you'd have several. You'd have TV programs also. The Community Voice would be a weekly newspaper, much thicker, with color photos. A big office, with a paid staff.

You'd inspire the young. From all my exerpeinces, whites-Jews have done nothing but fight against me for having a higher intellect, while pretending otherwise. They've hated me, because they've invested so much in my inferiority. They also hate me for not serving them, for having my own mind, for not speaking in that drone voice, non-offending, pacifying style you find in the black geldings they like and promote.

But by investing in yourselves, you'll be different. You will encourage black achievements in "non-black" fields. Most importantly, you'll have the AUTHORITY which you now lack. You make no sense at all. You tell young blacks that whites are against them, their traditional enemies. Yet, you tell them to go to their enemies for their survival and livelihoods!! You claim to be the blacks' "people" and natural friends, yet you absolutely refuse to support them in their livelihoods!!!

Try programming a computer with such logic. No computer or machine can operate with such a blatant contradiction. Therefore, I really don't have any time for your senseless Bullshit which has and continues to kill so many blacks. I don't support this outrage at all, and I have no reason to meet or socialize with such God-awful, murderous and phoney people as yourselves.

When you've had enough, and realize WHAT your so-called "leaders" have been doing to you, while you've been lying on your stomachs in their beds, then you will say, "No More." You'll get up and out. You'll denounce them, and Drive Them Out! Those are my terms.

"If ye suffer," the Buddha said, "ye suffer because of yourself."

The Negro Misleaders
Must Go!

LETTER[3]

Genetically What?..

Newsweek magazine has decided to put on its Front Cover the latest "proof" of the genetic intellectual inferiority of blacks, presenting the work of some d-g who's published a book on the subject.

1) I haven't read either Newsweek's article(s) or the book. But it doesn't matter. That's because you can be CERTAIN that no really scientific research has been done. To prove blacks' genetic inferiority in a scientific manner, then the same types of procedures must be carried out here as in all other scientific experiments.

There have to be both control and test groups, tracked over a period of time. For example, take 200 randomly selected blacks who perform poorly on IQ tests. Divide them equally into two groups. The control group you do absolutely nothing with, let them proceed as normal.

The test group of 100 you apply all sorts of training, teaching, coaching, provide learning skills and practice tests taking, over and over again on IQ and other tests, and most importantly provide immediate material incentives for success. Moreover, this test group must be supervised by properly funded black nationalist forces who will teach, instruct and nourish the blacks along the lines they believe to be important. Not the King Negroes, for reasons I don't have the space to explain here.

One should carry out this experiment on a group for at least 2 years. There should also be additional groups as variations of the social components of the above random test group, e.g. variations as to economic background, age, sex, parental situation, etc. Furthermore, since this is supposed to be a genetic issue, national boundaries can't be barriers. Test groups of blacks all throughout Africa, the Caribbean and South America must be included.

Perhaps in all one will have 10,000 or more below average scoring blacks, divided evenly into control and tet groups, being tracked.

Then after four or five years one can announce the first Preliminary results: If the d-g's point of view is scientifically correct, there should not appear any real difference between the IQ scores of the control groups vs. the test groups. The d-g's theory demands there is simply nothing teachings, material incentives, knowledge of African/black achievements, etc., can do to significantly raise IQ scores.

I haven't read Newsweek because I know such scientific experiments have not been conducted. Period. I DEFY AND CHALLENGE THE SCIENTIFIC COMMUNITY TO DENY THAT THIS OR A SIMILAR PROCEDURE IS ABSOLUTELY NECESSARY TO ASCERTAIN - IF AT ALL - DIFFICULT ISSUES CONCERNING GENETIC VS. SPIRITUAL/MORAL AND CULTURAL INTELLIGENCE.

2) There's lot more to be said, of course, but why should I both waste my time but more importantly fall into the white-Jews' trap they've again spunned? I just mentioned the above to throw the ball back into their court, and, to instantaneously and without further ado, totally obliterate any such claims by the d-g to having "scientific results."

3) But why do I say this is a trap spunned by the whites-Jews? because it's designed to get blacks to debating and arguing this crap. To place blacks on the defensive, and, to excuse the white-Jews' failure in partnership with their paid-for Negro misleaders.

Wake Up! The media is very controlled. The only issues that get debated are issues they want debated. Or, there're news events which they can't control, but the reporting and opinions about they do control.

Wake Up! All those matters which the white-Jews in the country are seriously against, they never debate. They never allow on the air, or talk shows. Or, if so, very limitedly and obliquely. Examples: a) You've never seen communists and socialists debate issues and their platforms. Before coming to Lexington, I lived for several years in Paris, France. There communists and socialists are seen daily on news, as well as their opposites, the French racist rightwing. It's called democracy. Indeed, the President of France is a Socialist, something impossible to imagine in America. America is against socialism/communism and so their ideas are never debated.

b) Jewish financial holdings and control - a very delicate issue with Jews because it has been an excuse for anti-Jewish reaction, just like blacks' alleged inferiority and black crime issues which have been used by anti-black forces. You've never seen an article or news program documenting Jewish financial and institutional controls.

Farrakhan's well-documented book from Jewish sources, "The Secret Relationship Between Blacks and Jews," was never reviewed in Newsweek or any other whites-Jews' controlled media, much less given a front cover. America is against anti-Jewish sentiments and makes sure that except for hearing about Hitler's holocaust there's no intellectual, scholarly or scientific debate about Jewish holdings and control - none whatsoever!

c) I have blasted the homosexuals, who've made their gains through debate in the media. But there's a segment of their movement, which presently, but only presently, America is against. That is, satan needs to first cement its gains with the acceptance of homosexuality itself, before it presents this other segment for debate. That segment is the homosexual pedophiles, of which Michael Jackson is an alleged representative.

The homosexual pedophiles, however, despite all sorts of efforts, don't get a chance to debate their offensive lies at all. I haven't heard these pedophiles' argument, but you can be certain they include identifying their movement with the black struggle!

4) Now, if you can't add 2+2, then this lesson should tell you a lot about how these whites-Jews, whom you thought were your friends, have played you. It should tell you everything you need to know of what they're not against, and who they are against.

They're against you, fool.

Therefore, the blacks should not see this Newsweek front cover story taunting black's inferiority as a revanche of the 1970's Shockeley debates and prior. This is not a call for black academics and intellectuals to "prove" this crap wrong, or show how intelligent the black debaters are. Once again. Blacks' attention and energies need to be focussed on investing one billion dollars a week into themselves.

Because what does a proof mean, anyhow? Whenever whites-Jews want to stab blacks again in a very sensitive area - this d-g's theory is just a remodel of the doctrine blacks aren't even human beings - then they will. This monster theory has more lives han a Freddy Kruger sequel. "Did you miss me?" Kruger asks in the current TV ads announcing his return.

5) Rather, to stop these sequels forever, the tables must be turned on the whites-Jews. Two things should be presented: i) A demand for the bank transfer of the first $50 million to black nationalist forces to finance their proper and necessary role in a real scientific project, as outlined above, to determine the truth of the d-g's theory, and,

ii) A demand for the scientific evaluation of, conversely, the genetic intellectual superiority of the Jews. Specifically, we want published the Jew's superior financial holdings and institutional control in America. The Jews' role in every major historical event. Farrakhan's book must be given serious and front cover attention.

This includes the Jew's pivotal role in every financial disaster and scam, like Solomon Brothers' manipulations which precipitated the Great Depression on Wall Street, or the Boeskys and Milkins. We want displayed the superior Jewish genes who operating internationally have been able to dupe and reduce the stupid natives, as they in superior fashion drained the natives' raw goods and wealth from them.

If this project is declared to be just an anti-Jewish project, we say that's really silly and ridiculous. It's scientific. Besides, we're taunting Jewish superiority. Not, as with the whites-Jews' d-g's theory, publishing about the quasi-human and inferiority of the blacks. Anti-Jewish? Don't be silly. Everybody wants to be superior. No?

The Negro Misleaders Must Go!

Don Steele

Lexington

NOTES

1. Printed December 2, 1994.

2. Printed December 16, 1994.

3. Printed October 28, 1994.